Marketing Research the R

MARKETING RESEARCH THE RIGHT WAY

A Harvard Business Review Paperback

Harvard Business Review paperback No. 90061

ISBN 0-87584-276-3

The *Harvard Business Review* articles in this collection are available individually. Discounts apply to quantity purchases. For information and ordering contact Operations Department, Harvard Business School Publishing Division, Boston, MA 02163. Telephone: (617) 495-6192, 9 a.m. to 5 p.m. EST. Fax: (617) 495-6985, 24 hours a day.

© 1975, 1983, 1985, 1986, 1987, 1988, 1989, 1990, 1991 by the President and Fellows of Harvard College.

Editor's Note: Some articles in this book may have been written before authors and editors began to take into consideration the role of women in management. We hope the archaic usage representing all managers as male does not detract from the usefulness of the collection.

All rights reserved. No part of this book may be reproduced, stored in a retrieval system, or transmitted, in any form or by any means, electronic, mechanical, photocopying, recording, or otherwise without the prior written permission of the copyright holder.
Printed in the United States of America by Harvard University, Office of the University Publisher.
93 92 91   5 4 3 2 1

Contents

The Market Research Encyclopedia
Vincent P. Barabba
3

Because market research is increasingly complicated, there is a need for a blueprint outlining major steps and questions. This foldout article provides a comprehensive protocol for research.

The New Product Development Map
Steven C. Wheelwright and W. Earl Sasser, Jr.
14

A technique for mapping product line "family trees" that can help coordinate market planning and research with product development.

Four Steps to Forecast Total Market Demand
F. William Barnett
29

Without a total-demand forecast, you're operating in the dark. This forecast can shed unexpected light on your strategy decisions.

New Gold Mines and Minefields in Market Research
Leonard M. Lodish and David J. Reibstein
35

Technology aids offer more precise consumer data than ever before—to marketers who understand the hazards.

"Backward" Market Research
Alan R. Andreasen
43

Managers and researchers must collaborate on research design in order to gather usable data. Knowing where you want to go and how to get there can pay off in research results that point to action.

Cost-Conscious Marketing Research
Alan R. Andreasen
47

Marketing research doesn't have to be complicated or expensive to be effective. Managers can benefit from alternative forms of research that are tailored to their needs and budgets.

Market Research the Japanese Way
Johny K. Johansson and Ikujuro Nonaka
51

The Japanese trust their instincts first, then turn to surveys. Staying close to the consumer—through strong vertical integration and a close watch on distribution channels—often pays off in impressive market shares.

When, Where, and How to Test Market
N.D. Cadbury
55

Field-tested guidelines to help managers decide essential questions about test marketing and how to evaluate the results.

The Case of the Test Market Toss-up
Steven H. Star and Glen L. Urban
65

Should Paradise Foods put its new frozen dessert on ice?

The Market Research Encyclopedia

by Vincent P. Barabba

To market well, you have to satisfy and at times exceed the expectations of the customer. But how do you know what the customer wants?

According to the textbooks, market research ought to provide the answer. Unfortunately, because of the way most traditional marketing research is conducted, it has fallen short of this important objective. At the core of the problem is the practice of using marketing research to confirm that a decision already made is the right decision rather than using market research to identify alternative choices and to support the process by which the best alternative is chosen.

In this series of foldout tables, I present a guide for managers who want to use market research to develop and support market-based decisions. The tables form a decision-support framework that uses research tools to help companies develop a balanced approach to the "technology push/demand pull" product development process. The structural components of the framework are accountable management, the company's decision process, marketplace reality, and the market research function.

The five sections of the gatefold identify the steps researchers must take: (1) Assess market information needs; (2) Measure the marketplace; (3) Store, retrieve, and display the data; (4) Describe and analyze market information; (5) Evaluate the research and assess its usefulness. The reference material here is encyclopedic—the product of a great deal of thought by colleagues in business, market research and advertising agencies, academia, and elsewhere. As such, the tables are invaluable for all stakeholders within the company who need to develop a sensitivity to the voice of the market. These stakeholders include people in product development, engineering, manufacturing, finance, human resources, and so forth.

Though the tables envision the "product" as a manufactured and engineered good, any manager can apply this decision-support framework to intangible products or services as well. The goal of customer satisfaction through an understanding of what the market wants and will pay for is, after all, the same.

Augmenting the tables are both a glossary of technical terms and a list of references, which is keyed at the bottom of each table by the authors' names.

Vincent P. Barabba is executive director of market research and planning at General Motors Corporation. He has had long experience developing knowledge for decision making, having served twice as director of the U.S. Census Bureau and in market research capacities at Xerox and Eastman Kodak. He is also president of the American Statistical Association.

		Review Information About Marketplace: Customers, Corporation, Legislature, Competitors		Interpret Marketplace Sig
Decision Makers	**Other Users**	**Current Influences**	**Future Influences**	
nd needed quality/value of information		Image studies by mail or telephone, involving financial leaders, legislators, and other politicians	Discussions with thought leaders, groups, think tanks, and innovators	Using qualitative research, determine meaning of signal. reasons for them
				Possibly use expert surveys/studies
		Competitive assessment studies	Development of regressions, and trend analyses scenarios	Use consumer studies
				Do studies on factors related signals
Use regular channels for requests Plan periodic research		At least every quarter or with major changes in the environment	Continuously, or at least prior to start of new product/service program	Continuously, or with a signi change in the environment
ity		1-3 months	3-6 months	Depends on complexity of p could be lengthy
		Product engineering	Strategic planners	Product engineering
		Technical staff	Marketing planners	Technical staff
		Product design	Economists	Product design
		Quality/reliability staff	Designers	Quality/reliability staff
		Sales management	Engineers	Sales management
		Product/service planning		Product/service planning
		Other staffs, including public relations, government relations, financial, and environmental activities		Outside experts
		Image ratings from financial leaders, and politicians	Trends in demographic, psycho-graphic, economic, environmental, regulatory, and legislative factors	Data containing signals plu qualitative data to interpret
		Competitors' plans	Company capabilities assessment	Extensive market/sales dat
	→	$10,000-$100,000 (for initial data collection)	Depends on level of effort and breadth of product line	Depends on complexity ($10,000-$100,000 for int collection)
	→	Develops and adjusts company policies and programs	Required for product/service development	Determines direction of proc and programs
		Boyd, Westfall, and Stasch		

④ Describe and Analyze Market Information

	Descriptive Analysis	**Data Reduction**	**Inference**	**Predict**
Examples of Analysis Techniques	Mean	Factor analysis	Hypothesis testing	Conjoint
	Variance	Principal components analysis	Regression	Regress
	Box plot	Multidimensional scaling		Box-Jer
	Correlations	Cluster analysis		Smooth
	Graphic analysis	Product position maps		
When to Undertake Activity	←———————————————— In response to requests ————————————————			
	←———————————————— As part of ongoing market research analysis ————			
	Before data reduction	Before inference activity	Before prediction and decision-making activities	Before
	As part of exploratory activity	As part of exploratory analysis	In special studies	In spec
Time required	Minimal; depends on the quantity of data and analysis package	1-2 weeks (more than descriptive analysis)	1 week to several months, depending on messiness of the data, complexity of the problem, depth of analysis required, and time horizon of the problem	Can be fast on activiti
Collaboration Required	None	With builders of database and users of information	With data providers and information users; can be extensive	With u compa Possib
Data and/or Sample Size Required	Values of the observed variables	Fairly large sample size	Data collected that are relevant to analysis	May re analysi inferen
Expected Output	Summary of data	Maps Knowledge of structure of underlying relationships in the data	Input to prediction and decision making	Data or their lik
Importance	Simple overview of data	Gives insight into structure of data	Knowledge about structural relationships among variables	Output thinking May affe resource

References

	Prepare Early Mock-Up Tables	Display Information	Prepare Documentation	Train Users
	Early in the process, prepare expected output tables to obtain user groups' reactions	For some applications, readily understood software packages such as MacDraw, Tell-A-Graf, Atlas, or Page Maker are useful Computer use ranges from PCs to mainframes	For: Data collection System File contents Analysis Display of information	Users must know how to manipulate data, prepare graphics, understand statistical and analytical techniques used, and present data effectively so that they can benefit fully
	As early as possible and ongoing	After analysis to enhance written report During analysis of data	From database development onward	Initially and as needed
	Several days spread over several months Variable and depending on the requirements	Short if staff has training in display packages (depends on necessary detail)	Long; enough to budget for Depends on complexity and quantity of data	Not as much time as other efforts Time is front-loaded
	Before complete analysis, present to expected users to determine usefulness	With system users so that they understand system capabilities With researchers to ensure correct presentation With suppliers	With data suppliers	User feedback is necessary
	Collaboration with users Clear presentation of hypothetical output in expected format	Ensure clarity to user of output device and analysis and graphics techniques Graphic display capability Menu driven; standardized report materials	Electronic access to documentation Easily understood documentation	Equipment Instructional materials relevant to users' needs
		presentations, decision trees, tables, maps	Documentation on file contents, on method of use of equipment and analysis techniques, and on analysis interpretation	A confident and skilled user community that can use data effectively and efficiently
		Cleveland; Schmid	Review existing documentation for similar applications	

③ Store, Retrieve, and Display the Data

	Store Information	**Retrieve Information**	**Reformat Data**
Description	Preparation of data-delivery specifications Creation of new variables for permanent storage Storage of new and cleaned data	Run computer programs or packages to retrieve data	Reformat from data's r... meet organizational ob... requirements Includes cleaning, cod... checking the data
When to Undertake Activity	Data-delivery specifications prepared before data collection Creation of variables and data storage begin after data collection	Routinely and as needed	As soon as data are re...
Time Required	Extensive; influenced by quantity of collected information	Time needed to run program	Much time needed to c... and check the data
Collaboration Required	System users with data providers	System users to define needs	With system users and providers
Requirements	User friendly Effective Consistent across data sets Mergeable Trackable User transparent	Standardized retrieval package Transparent file linkages Menu approach Electronic selection assistance Meaningful and functional file prefixes User can write own programs Fast retrieval capability Cost effective User friendly Can download to a PC environment	Standardized applicati... Meets user needs for s... well as general applica... Common format, men... allow retrieval for obse... analysis User friendly Flexible to allow for use... range of skills Self-explanatory names... variables Easily understood outp... Database/system comp...
Expected Output	User-friendly database	Data, charts, comparisons, tables, maps	Reformatted, clean data Manipulatable data to c... required information
Cost	Variable, depending on the quality and quantity of data, system they are resident on, communication link... For some repetitive efforts, initial costs may be higher than later costs Cost considerations should include the value added of the data considered		
References	← Company's own market informatio...		

⑤ Evaluate the Research and Assess Its Usefulness

	Decision Making
lysis	Bayesian statistics
	Decision analysis
	→
	→
on making	Before commitment of major resources
dies	
extensive but also very etion of previous	Varies; may range from minutes to months
analyses and keholders	With decision makers, company stakeholders, and data providers
builders of database	
output from descriptive a reduction, or	Output of inference and prediction activities
ible alternatives and utcomes	Commitment of resources
cause revision of	Crucial to survival of organization
location of capital	
kins; Newbold; Rubinfeld;	French; Holtzman; McClave and Benson; Smith

	Action Audits	**Simulation of Final Results**
Description	For each contemplated action, develop a set of research questions to determine its soundness	Prepare mock-up of fin presentation using sim findings presented as actual findings will be
When to Undertake Activity	Start of the research project	Before data collection
Time Required	1-2 hours	8 hours for researcher 2 hours for managers
Collaboration Required	Managers with researchers	Managers with researc
Data Required	None	Simulated
Expected Output	Inventory of possible actions	Mock-up of alternative Rehearsal of research-
Clarity of Expected Output	High; explicit statements of plans	High
Cost	No out-of-pocket cost	Managers: no out-of-p Researchers: 1 day of if outside supplier is us
Frequency of Use	Moderate	Low
Principal Benefits	More relevant and more actionable research Faster use of research	Clearer sense of issues More relevant research and final data More useful research r
Principal Limitations and Obstacles	None Managers may be unwilling to disclose possible actions to researchers	None Time required may be extensive
References	←	

	Discrepancy Analysis	Insurance Premium Calculation	Information as Arbitration	Assess Market Research Project
	Predict research findings, compare them later with actual findings High levels of discrepancy between the two indicate usefulness of findings	Research determines if the cost of a wrong decision, weighted by its likelihood, is greater than the cost of the research Serves as insurance against wrong decision	Market research information is used to reconcile differences among functional areas	Information is dysfunctional if technically flawed, misleading, irrelevant, poorly presented, incorrectly interpreted, or deliberately misconstrued
	Before final data are distributed to managers	As part of decision whether to do research	After research is completed	After research is completed
	½ hour of manager time; 1 hour of researcher time	Less than ½ hour	½ hour per decision maker	½ hour per participant Corresponding time of an auditor
	Among managers	Among managers	Managers with auditor	Managers with qualified auditor
	None	Cost of research and approximate cost of an unsuccessful action	None	None
	Comparison of managers' expectations with actual results	Ratio indicating desirability of doing research	Qualitative assessment	Qualitative assessments by auditor
	High	Mixed; ratio is specific, its interpretation less so	Moderate to high	Moderate
	No out-of-pocket cost	No out-of-pocket cost	No out-of-pocket cost If outside auditor is used, 1 day	No out-of-pocket cost If outside auditor is used, 1 day
	Low	Moderate	Low	Low
	Gives a measure of the value of information Reduces "I told you so" behavior	Guideline concerning potential value of doing research	Better understanding and appreciation of the role of research	Guidelines for improving research-use process
	None Managers' reluctance to admit uncertainty	None Difficulty in calculating cost of an error	Difficult to get managers to reflect on changes in their perspectives Managers may not want research in an arbitration role	Securing candid assessments from managers Managers' reluctance to disclose abuse of research

Barabba and Zaltman; Zaltman and Deshpande; Zaltman

	Nonprobabilistic Data			
	Mixed Mode	**Convenience Samples**	**Focus Group**	**Central Location Interviewing (Product Clinics)**
	Combination of mail, telephone, or in-person survey	Administered to respondents recruited on-site in high-traffic areas or from existing groups	Small discussion led by a facilitator	Respondents come to a central location to evaluate products
	Self-administered Paper and pencil CATI CAPI	Computerized Paper and pencil Self-administered In trailer, van, rented store, or street location	Discussion Audiovisual Tape recorder Focus group room/facility with one-way glass preferred	Self-administered Personal interviews Computer administered Paper and pencil CAPI
	Combines advantages of different methods Creates flexibility in amount and detail of information collected	Probably less expensive than other methods Fast	Group synergy generated Encourages brainstorming Respondents discuss issues in their own words	Gives product feedback from static or dynamic evaluation under controlled conditions Allows respondent exposure to actual product Under certain conditions, a representative sample can be obtained and statistics generalized to the entire population
	Difficulty of getting high-quality list Potential for losing respondents between waves Potential for differential impact of mode on responses Combines expenses of two modes	High proportion of unrepresentative responses Information collected is more directive and suggestive than projective Ability to generalize results is limited Survey must be short and simple	Information collected is more directive and suggestive than projective Facilitator, vocal participants can dominate the results Ability to generalize results is limited	Very expensive Responses in this artificial environment may not reflect responses in the market Complicated logistics Development of test product can be time consuming and expensive
	65%–90%	Not applicable	Varies widely by topic and market	Tends to be low, though varies widely by product and market
	Depends on modes of data collection and percent collected by each	Varies widely	Varies widely	Generally quite expensive but varies widely
	Complete list of target population If this is an area probability sample, detailed geographic data are required	High-incidence location for target population	List of target population Sometimes organization lists of members can be used	List of target population
	Groves and Lepkowski — Bradburn and Sudman —	Dillon, Madden, and Firtle	Churchill	Churchill

Translate Users' Information Needs into Research Questions
Interviews
Careful probing
Determine issues, needs, timing, decisions affected by information produced, and impact
At start of research project and frequently thereafter
In meetings over the course of the project
A few hours to several months, depending on when output is required
Users and researchers must understand each other's requirements
Data containing signals plus qualitative data to interpret them
Extensive market/sales data
Cost of staff time
Crucial in ensuring communication among parties
Churchill; Zikmund

② Measure the Marketplace

Primary Data

Probabilistic Sample Surveys

	Mail	Telephone	In-Person
Description	Self-administered survey mailed to respondents	Administered over the telephone	Administered respondent's location
Implementation Technique	Self-administered Paper and pencil	CATI (computer-aided telephone interview) Respondents called from a phone-interview facility Audio taping	CAPI (comp interview) Paper and p Use visual a respondent t Audiovisual Private settin
Benefits	Least expensive probabilistic method Wide geographic coverage Large sample sizes	Fastest method Permits moderately lengthy questionnaires Flexible Lower item nonresponse rates Control over who responds Low chance of misinterpretation of questions	Highest resp Permits long interviews Lower item r Low chance questions Enables inte issues Can use avc products the
Limitations	List quality can vary Low response rates Introduces potential for bias Long field time Limited length and complexity of questionnaires Limited control over who completes survey High potential for item nonresponse No chance for interviewer to probe	Limited time Potential bias if topic is correlated with characteristics of no-phone households or unlisted numbers Unlisted and outdated phone numbers may reduce list quality Little time for respondents to ponder questions	Large field s data-collecti Potential for Outdated na phone numbe quality Expensive to interview
Response Rates Without Incentives	10%-85%	20%-85%	70%-90%
Cost per Completed Interview	$5-$10	$20-$90	$150-$400
Source of Sample	Complete, accurate list of the target population	Complete list of target population Use of random digit dialing is possible if list is unavailable	Complete list If this is an ar detailed geog required
References	Dillman	Groves et al.	Kish

Glossary

Bayesian Statistics: Statistical methods that incorporate prior judgment into problems of inference.

Box-Jenkins: A forecasting method based on time series models that relies on the ability to capture the trend, cycles, and other characteristics of the time series systematically.

Box Plots: Graphic techniques that provide information about central tendency, variability, and shape of distribution of data.

Cluster Analysis: A statistical analysis that groups people or objects on the basis of common characteristics.

Conjoint Analysis: Models and techniques that emphasize the transformation of subjective responses into estimated parameters.

Correlation: The extent or degree of statistical association among two or more variables.

Data Reduction: Methods of reducing large amounts of data into smaller groupings that reveal the structure and interdependencies of the data.

Decision Analysis: A logical and sequential process designed to yield high-quality decisions about complex problems with important uncertainties.

Descriptive Analysis: Use of statistics to describe the results of an experiment or investigation.

Factor Analysis: A set of statistical techniques that address themselves to the study of interrelationships among a total set of observed variables.

Hypothesis Testing: A general term referring to the procedures for the statistical determination of the validity of an hypothesis.

Multidimensional Scaling: A body of techniques for representing graphically the locations and interrelationships among a set of points.

Nonprobabilistic Sample Surveys: Surveys not based on a probability sample of the population.

Prediction: Development of definite statements about the future based on a knowledge of how changes in the environment will shape the future.

Primary Data: Data collected for a specific issue under consideration.

Principal Components Analysis: A statistical technique that reduces a large number of variables into a much smaller number of dimensions or factors that can account for a reasonable proportion of the variance among all the original variables.

Probability Sampling: The process of selecting elements or groups of elements from a well-defined population by a procedure that gives each element a calculable nonzero probability of inclusion in the sample.

Product Position Maps: Maps that represent the perceived relationships among brands, with shorter distances between brands indicating greater similarity in perception of relevant attributes (see Multidimensional Scaling and Principal Components Analysis).

Regression: A statistical analysis tool that quantifies the relationship between a dependent variable and one or more independent variables.

Secondary Data: Information originally compiled for a purpose other than the one under consideration.

Smoothing Technique: A technique that uses a series of historical data to predict the value of some future event in the series. The process assumes that there is some pattern in the series that will repeat.

Statistical Inference: A method of judging the validity of a statistical hypothesis about a statistical population based on a sample.

Variance: The extent to which a random variable or statistic is dispersed about its mean value.

Author's note: I thank Barbara C. Richardson for her assistance in putting these tables together.

① Assess Market Information Needs

	Decision Analysis	**Assess User Needs Continuously**		
		Strategic Planning Group	**Product Planning Group**	**Market Analysts**
Description	Frame the decision to be made	User/provider meeting to identify issues/uncertainties and lead to research questions, timing decisions, assessme...		
	Determine most important uncertainties	Needs define type of research		
		Process should lead to full analysis plan		
	Obtain best judgments about the range of uncertainties	Before approving research, management should review issues, methods, anticipated results, analysis plan, and c...		
	Determine the need for and range of research			
When to Undertake Activity	Throughout information-needs assessment process	Regularly, before update of strategic plan	At stages in market planning process, including before concept initiation	As needed to respond to market events and anticipated internal actions
Time Required	Depends on the complexity of the decisions at hand	Varies from 1 to many meetings and 1 day to several months, depending on number of users, timing needs, and c...		
Collaboration Required	All knowledge producers and users with those assigned to decision analysis support	Involvement of user groups plus liaison with market research function and with management review		
Data Required	Information relevant to the decision at hand, determined during the analysis	Clearly defined plan or objectives with identified uncertainties that can be reduced		
		Clear relation between reducing uncertainty and resulting change		
		Timing until decision or action		
		Value of differences between alternative decisions		
Incremental Cost	Cost of staff time	◀──────────────── Nominal ────────────────		
Importance	Ensures that parties jointly determine information needs	◀──────────────── Most critical part of research		
References	Holtzman; Howard	Churchill; Kinnear and Taylor; Zikmund		

References

Vincent P. Barabba and Gerald Zaltman, *Market Based Decision Making* (Boston: Harvard Business School Press, forthcoming).

George E.P. Box and Gwilym M. Jenkins, *Time Series Analysis: Forecasting and Control*, revised edition (San Francisco: Holden Day, 1976).

Harper Boyd, Ralph Westfall, and Stanley Stasch, *Marketing Research: Text and Cases*, 5th ed. (Homewood, Ill.: Richard D. Irwin, 1981).

Norman M. Bradburn and Seymour Sudman, *Polls and Surveys* (San Francisco: Jossey-Bass, 1988).

Gilbert Churchill, Jr., *Marketing Research Methodological Foundations*, 4th ed. (Chicago: Dryden Press, 1984).

William Cleveland, *The Elements of Graphing Data* (Monterey, Calif.: Wadsworth Publishing, 1985).

Don A. Dillman, *Mail and Telephone Surveys* (New York: Wiley Interscience Publications, 1978).

W.R. Dillon, J. Madden, and N.H. Firtle, *Market Research in a Marketing Environment* (St. Louis, Mo.: Times-Mirror/Mosby College Publishing, 1987).

S. French, ed., *Readings in Decision Analysis* (New York: Chapman and Hall, 1989).

C.W. J. Granger and Paul Newbold, *Forecasting Economic Time Series* (San Diego: Academic Press, 1977).

R.M. Groves and James M. Lepkowski, "Dual Frame Mixed Mode Survey Design," *Journal of Official Statistics*, 1985.

R.M. Groves et al., *Telephone Survey Methodology* (New York: John Wiley & Sons, 1988).

Joseph F. Hair, Jr., Rolph E. Anderson, and Ronald L. Tatham, *Multivariate Data Analysis with Readings*, 2d ed. (New York: Macmillan, 1987).

Samuel Holtzman, *Intelligent Decision System* (Reading, Mass.: Addison-Wesley, 1989).

Ronald A. Howard, "Decision Analysis: Practice and Promise," *Management Science*, vol. 34, no. 6, June 1988.

Thomas C. Kinnear and James R. Taylor, *Marketing Research*, 3d ed. (New York: McGraw-Hill, 1987).

Leslie Kish, *Survey Sampling* (New York: John Wiley & Sons, 1965).

J. T. McClave and P. G. Benson, *Statistics for Business and Economics*, 4th ed. (San Francisco: Dellery Publishers, 1988).

Robert S. Pindyck and Daniel L. Rubinfeld, *Econometric Models and Economic Forecasts* (New York: McGraw-Hill, 1981).

Calvin F. Schmid, *Statistical Graphics: Design Principles and Practices* (New York: John Wiley & Sons, 1983).

J.Q. Smith, *Decision Analysis: A Bayesian Approach* (New York: Chapman and Hall, 1987).

George W. Snedecor and William G. Cochran, *Statistical Methods*, 6th ed. (Ames: Iowa State University Press, 1967).

Gerald Zaltman, "The Management and Use of Market Research," presented at the Conference on Making More Effective Use of Market Information, April 12-13, 1989, Phoenix, Arizona, (Cambridge, Mass.: Marketing Science Institute).

Gerald Zaltman and Rohit Deshpande, "Increasing the Utilization of Scientific and Technical Information" in William R. King and Gerald Zaltman, eds., *Marketing Scientific and Technical Information* (Boulder, Colo.: Westview Press, 1979).

William G. Zikmund, *Business Research Methods* (Chicago: Dryden Press, 1984).

*Mapping is a medium and also a message:
Get together on new products sooner and smarter with...*

The New Product Development Map

by Steven C. Wheelwright and W. Earl Sasser, Jr.

No business activity is more heralded for its promise and approached with more justified optimism than the development and manufacture of new products. Whether in mature businesses like automobiles and electrical appliances, or more dynamic ones like computers, managers correctly view new products as a chance to get a jump on the competition.

Ideally, a successful new product can set industry standards—standards that become another company's barrier to entry—or open up crucial new markets. Think of the Sony Walkman. New products are good for the organization. They tend to exploit as yet untapped R&D discoveries and revitalize the engineering corps. New product campaigns offer top managers opportunities to reorganize and to get more out of a sales force, factory, or field service network, for example. New products capitalize on old investments.

Perhaps the most exciting benefit, though, is the most intangible: corporate renewal and redirection. The excitement, imagination, and growth associated

 **Make new products build on your investments in R&D and sales.**

with the introduction of a new product invigorate the company's best people and enhance the company's ability to recruit new forces. New products build confidence and momentum.

Unfortunately, these great promises of new product development are seldom fully realized. Products half make it; people burn out. To understand why, let's look at some of the more obvious pitfalls.

1. *The moving target.* Too often the basic product concept misses a shifting market. Or companies may make assumptions about channels of distribution that just don't hold up. Sometimes the project gets

---

Steven C. Wheelwright and W. Earl Sasser, Jr. are both professors at the Harvard Business School. Mr. Wheelwright's research and teaching focus on new product and manufacturing process development. His latest book is Dynamic Manufacturing, *written with Robert H. Hayes and Kim B. Clark (Free Press, 1988). Mr. Sasser developed the first course on the management of service operations at HBS, and, with his colleague Daryl Wyckoff, he coauthored several books in the field of service management. Currently he is studying service quality, service productivity, internationalization of services, and service research and development.*

into trouble because of inconsistencies in focus; you start building a stripped-down version and wind up with a load of options. The project time lengthens, and longer projects invariably drift more and more from their initial target. Classic market misses include the Ford Edsel in the mid-1950s and Texas Instruments' home computer in the late 1970s. Even very successful products like Apple's Macintosh line of personal computers can have a rocky beginning.

2. *Lack of product distinctiveness.* This risk is high when designers fail to consider a full range of alternatives to meet customer needs. If the organization gets locked into a concept too quickly, it may not bring differing perspectives to the analysis. The market may dry up, or the critical technologies may be sufficiently widespread that imitators appear out of nowhere. Plus Development introduced Hardcard,® a hard disc that fits into a PC expansion slot, after a year and a half of development work. The company thought it had a unique product with at least a nine-month lead on competitors. But by the fifth day of the industry show where Hardcard® was introduced, a competitor was showing a prototype of a competing version. And within three months, the competitor was shipping its new product.

3. *Unexpected technical problems.* Delays and cost overruns can often be traced to overestimates of the company's technical capabilities or simply to its lack of depth and resources. Projects can suffer delays and stall mid-course if essential inventions are not completed and drawn into the designers' repertoire before the product development project starts. An industrial controls company we know encountered both problems: it changed a part from metal to plastic only to discover that its manufacturing processes could not hold the required tolerances and also that its supplier could not provide raw material of consistent quality.

4. *Mismatches between functions.* Often one part of the organization will have unrealistic or even impossible expectations of another. Engineering may design a product that the company's factories cannot produce, for example, or at least not consistently at low cost and with high quality. Similarly, engineering may design features into products that marketing's established distribution channels or selling approach cannot exploit. In planning its requirements, manufacturing may assume an unchanging mix of new products, while marketing mistakenly assumes that manufacturing can alter its mix dramatically on short notice. One of the most startling mismatches we've encountered was created by an aerospace company whose manufacturing group built an assembly plant too small to accommodate the wingspan of the plane it ultimately had to produce.

Thus new products often fail because companies misunderstand the most promising markets and channels of distribution and because they misapprehend their own technological strengths or the product's technological challenges. Nothing can eliminate all the risks, but clearly the most important thing to do early on when developing a new product is to get all contributors to the process communicating: marketing with manufacturing, R&D with both. Products fail from a lack of planning; planning fails from a lack of information.

Developing a new generation of products is a lot like taking a journey into the wilderness. Who would dream of setting off without a map? Of course, you would try to clarify the purpose of the journey and make sure that needed equipment is available and in order. But once committed to the trip, you need a map of the terrain, something everybody can study – the focus for discussion, the basis for planning alternative courses. Knowing where you've come from and where you are is essential to knowing how to get where you want to go.

Mapping Existing Products

We have often used this analogy of a map with corporate managers involved in product development, and gradually it became clear to us that an actual map is needed, not just an analogy. Managers need a way to see the evolution of a company's product lines – the "where we are" – in order to expose the markets and technologies that have been driving the evolution – the "where we've come from." Such a map presents the evolution of current product lines in a summary yet strikingly clear way so that all functional areas in the organization can respond to a common vision. The map provides a basis for sharing information. And by enabling managers to compare the assumptions underlying current product lines with the ideal assumptions of new research, it points to new market opportunities and technological challenges. Why, for example, should an organization build for department stores when specialty discount outlets are the emerging channels of distribution? Why bend metals when you can mold ceramics?

The first exhibit illustrates a generic map that indicates how the product offerings in one generation may be related to each other. These relations

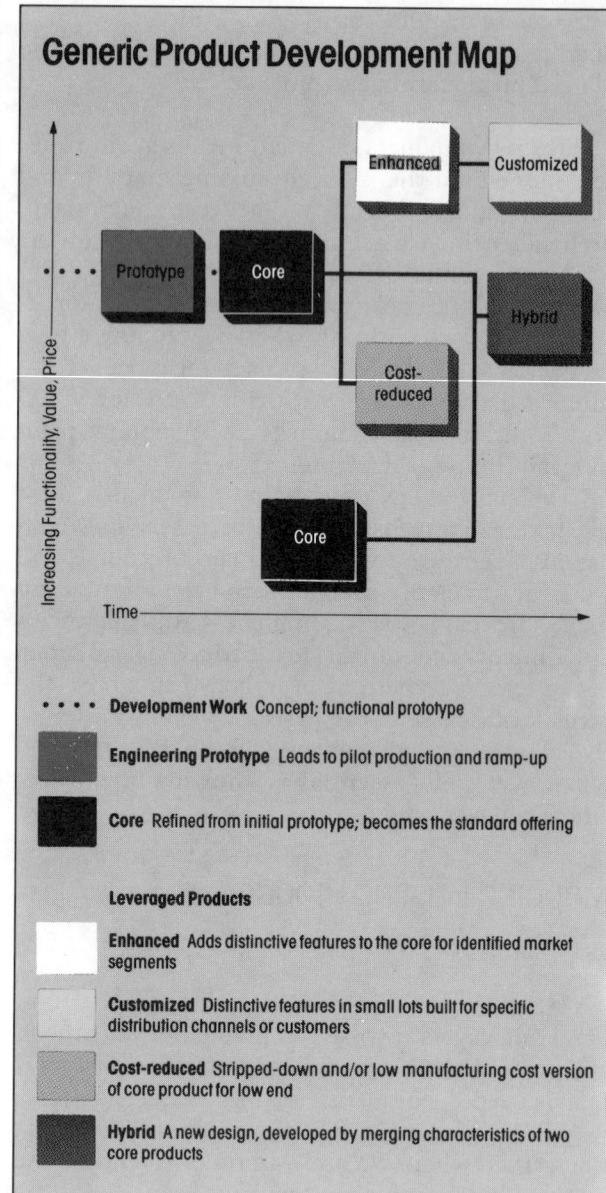

against which consumers compare the rest of the product line.

Enhanced products, in red, are developed from the core design; distinctive features are added for various, more discriminating markets. Enhanced products are the first products leveraged from the capabilities put in place to produce the core and the first aimed at new or extended market opportunities. Often companies even identify them as enhanced versions, for example, IBM's DisplayWrite 3.1 is an enhanced version of DisplayWrite 3. But a leveraged product isn't necessarily more costly: the idea is simply to get more out of a fixed process—more "bang for the buck." As companies leverage high-end products,

"Leveraged" products show what you know — and had better know.

they may customize them in smaller lots for specific channels or to give consumers more choice (shown in blue). The cost-reduced model, shown in green, starts with essentially the same technology and design as the core product but is a stripped-down version, often with less expensive materials and lower factory costs, aimed at a price-sensitive market. (Think of the old Chevrolet Biscayne, which was many times the vehicle of choice for taxicabs and business fleets.)

Finally, there is the hybrid product (shown in purple), developed out of two cores. The initial two-stage thermostat products—accommodating a daytime and nighttime temperature setting—were hybrids of a traditional thermostat product and high-end, programmable thermostat lines.

On the generic map, from left to right is calendar time, and from bottom to top designates lower to higher added value or functionality, which usually also means a shift from cheaper to more expensive products.

These distinctions—core, hybrid, and the others—are immediately useful because they give managers a way of thinking about their products more rigorously and less anecdotally. But the various turns on the product map—the various "leverage points"—also serve as crucial indicators of previous management assumptions about the corporate strengths and market forces shaping product evolutions.

A map that shows a proliferation of enhanced products toward the high end, for example, says something important about the market opportunities managers identified after they had introduced the core. A map's configuration raises necessary ques-

are the building blocks that allow us to track the evolution of product families from one generation to another.

The map categorizes product offerings (and the development efforts they entail) as "core" and "leveraged" products, and divides leveraged products into "enhanced," "customized," "cost reduced," and "hybrid" products. (These designations seem to cover most cases, but managers should feel free to add whatever other categories they need.) A core product, first in gray for the engineering prototype, then in black, is the engineering platform, providing the basis for further enhancements. The core product is the initial, standard product introduced. It changes little from year to year and is often the benchmark

CHARTS BY DIANE McCAFFERY

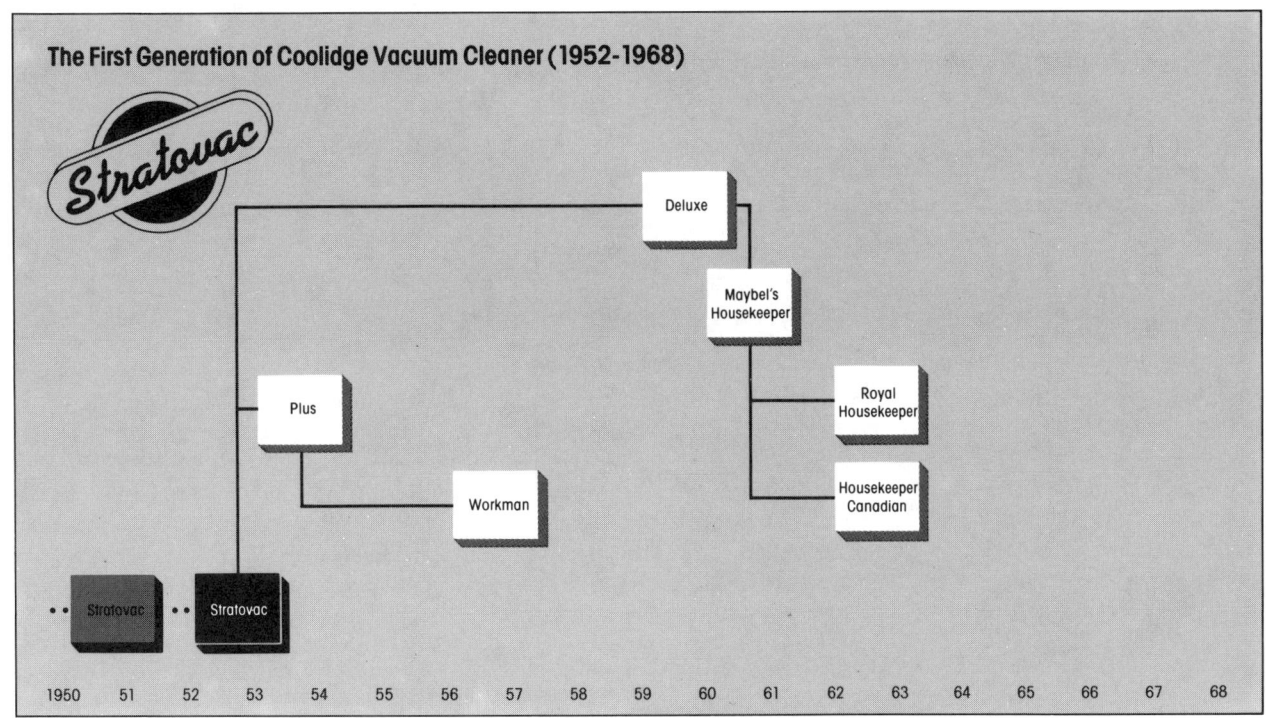

tions about dominant channels of distribution – then and now. That products could have been leveraged in particular ways, moreover, says something important about in-house technological and manufacturing capabilities – capabilities that may still exist or may need changing. The map generates the right discussions. When managers know how and why they have leveraged products in the past, they know better how to leverage the company in the present.

The First Generation

How can managers plan, develop, and position a set of products – that is, how do they build a dynamic map? With the generic map in mind, let us track offerings from generation to generation, as shown in the second exhibit. Imagine a very simple line of vacuum cleaners, Coolidge Corporation's "Stratovac," introduced, say, in 1952. The core product, the Stratovac, was a canister-type appliance with a 2.5 horsepower motor. Constructed mainly from cut and stamped metals, it was distributed through department stores and hardware chains.

The following year, reaching for the somewhat more affluent suburban household, Coolidge brought out the "Stratovac Plus," an enhanced Stratovac delivered in a choice of three colors, with a 4 horsepower motor and a recoiling cord. In 1959, the company introduced the "Stratovac Deluxe" – a Stratovac Plus with a vacuum resistance sensor (which cut off the power when the bag was full) and a power head with a rotating brush for deep pile or shag carpeting. By 1959, the basic Stratovac cost $89, the Stratovac Plus, $109, and the Stratovac Deluxe, $159.

To reach the industrial market at $79, Coolidge had decided to offer the "Stratovac Workman," a stripped-down Plus model – one color, no recoiling cord. That was introduced in 1956. And when Deluxe sales rocketed, Coolidge offered Maybel's department store chain a customized version of it, the Stratovac "Maybel's Housekeeper." This came out in 1960, in Maybel's blue gray, with the power head. The price was "only" $129. (Coolidge eventually customized the "Housekeeper Canadian" for the Simpton's chain in Canada, and the "Royal Housekeeper" for the Mid-Lakes chain in England.)

Again, this is a simple product line, but even so, the map raises interesting questions, especially for younger managers who came after this era. Why the Stratovac Plus? Why a proliferation of products toward the high end?

In fact, during the 1950s, most companies marketed home appliances through department stores with product families visibly shaped by the distribution channels. Products stood side by side in the stores, to be demonstrated by a salesperson. The markup was similar for each product on the floor.

What differentiated products in product families at the time was an appliance manufacturer's reach to

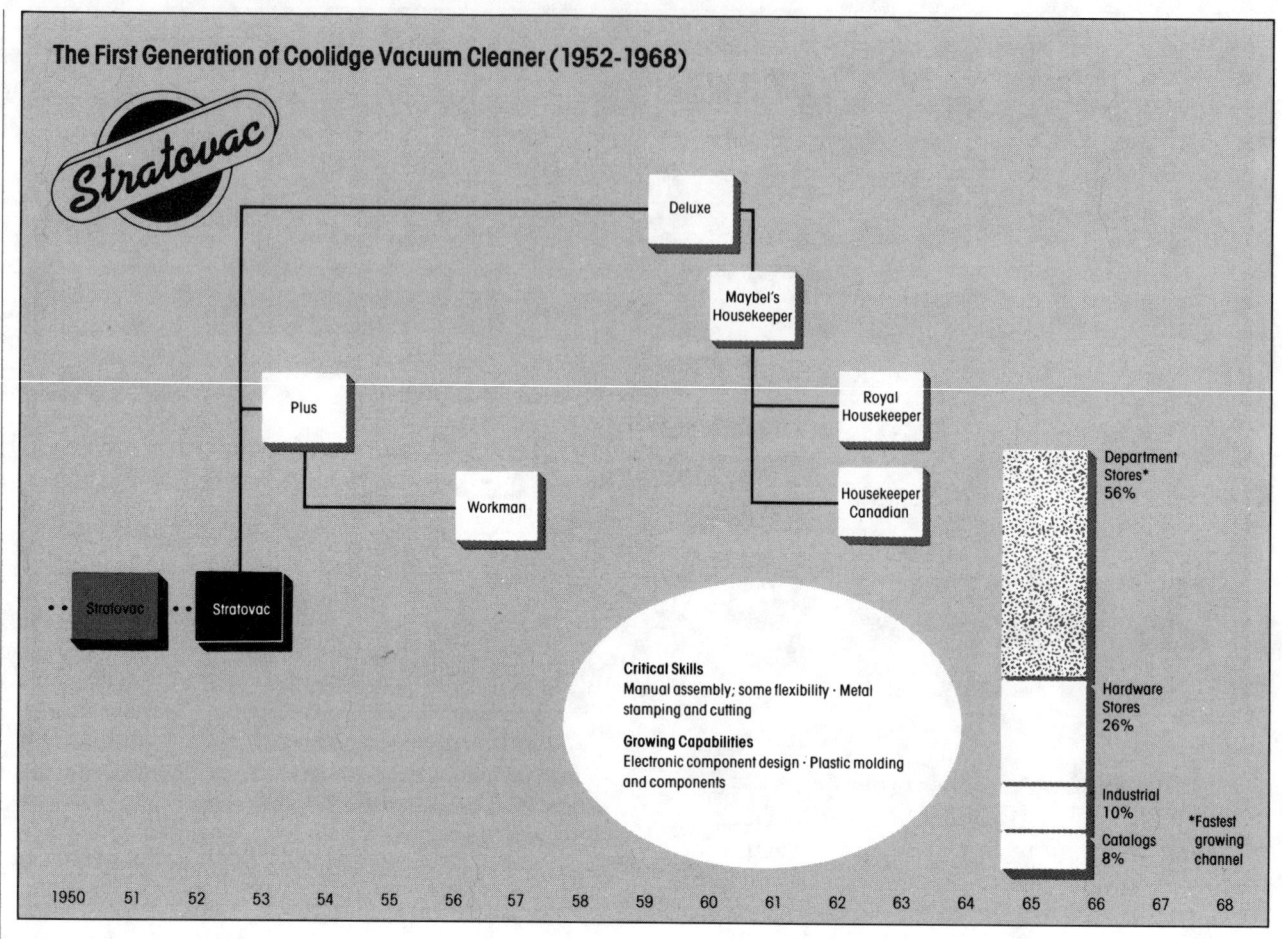

satisfy more or less obvious customer segments—customers differentiated by factors like income and marital status. (In the 1950s, most vacuum cleaner purchasers were women, with more or less money, time, and patience.)

How Coolidge leveraged its products also points to certain fixed—and not especially unique—manufacturing capabilities. During the 1950s, company engineers designed appliances for manual assembly and traditional notions of economies of scale. By the end of the 1950s, Coolidge acquired new vacuum sensor innovations from the auto industry. It also learned certain flexible manufacturing techniques, making different colors and options possible.

By 1958, Coolidge had solved most of the technical problems of the Stratovac line and had recruited a number of ambitious design engineers to integrate vacuum sensor and power heads into the line. The life cycle of the product—including development time, which stretched back to 1949—was typical for core products of that time: 10 to 15 years. Demand for the Stratovac remained strong throughout the 1950s, and Coolidge sold to department stores in roughly the same proportion as its competition, except for companies organized around the door-to-door trade.

The company's increased (and not fully utilized) technical competence and the steadiness of its key distribution channels are crucial pieces of information to add to the map (see the third exhibit). The map summarizes technical competence in the oval beneath the product lines, and Coolidge's gross sales by distribution channel in the box graph. The fastest growing distribution channel in the industry—in this case, department stores—is shaded for emphasis.

The Second Generation

With so much technical talent in-house, and a society growing increasingly affluent, Coolidge could not be expected to rest on the Stratovac's success indefinitely. Sales were steady, but by the mid-1960s customers assumed there would be some innovations. The age of plastics was dawning; the vanguard of the baby boom was taking apartments; it was the "new and improved" era.

Moreover, marketing people at Coolidge began to detect a new potential market at the low end. People who had relied on their Stratovacs for a decade were looking around for a second, lighter weight appliance for quick cleanups or for the workroom or garage. Lighter weight and cheaper naturally meant more reliance on plastic components.

In the early 1960s, Coolidge managers decided on two product families, each with its own core product (see the fourth exhibit). The design team that had brought out the old core Stratovac would handle the "Stratovac II," and company new hires would de-

Products are supposed to change as customers and distribution channels change.

sign a second line, the all-plastic, mass-produced "Handivac" ("any color, so long as it's beige").

The Stratovac II, introduced in 1968, was heavier and had a 4.3 horsepower motor, resulting in a slightly noisier operation, "jet noise," which the marketing people reasoned would actually increase respect for its power. Half of the case was now plastic for a "streamlined" appearance. The core Stratovac II boasted a new dust-bag system, which virtually eliminated the need for handling dust. A retractable cord was also standard.

The Stratovac II "Sentry," an enhanced version of the core, included electronic controls for variable speed and came in many colors. The Stratovac II "Imperial," like the old Deluxe model, came with the power head. The Stratovac II Workman continued to sell steadily to the light industrial market, as did the Stratovac II Housekeeper line to the department store chains that still sold the vast majority of units.

Most notable about the Stratovac II was how little changed it was, certainly on the manufacturing end. Assembly was still chiefly manual, along the lines of the 1950s – no priority given to modularity, design for manufacturability, or any of the considerations that would drive designers later on. There was some outsourcing of components to Mexico and Taiwan but no real attention to automation. The only significant change in the Stratovac II came in 1973, when inflationary pressures pushed management to develop a fully plastic casing and critical plastic components – in effect, a hybrid developed by merging technologies of the high-end vacuum cleaner with the low-end Handivac.

Handivac, the second core product, introduced in 1969, was something of a disappointment – mostly because of the inexperience of the team managing its development. Reliability was a problem, given Handivac's almost complete dependence on plastic components, components subjected to higher than expected temperatures from an old, slightly updated 2.5 horsepower motor. Weight was also a problem: it was not as light as promised. Mass-production lines, which were partially automated, were considered a success when they were finally debugged.

Perhaps the greatest problem with the Handivac, however, was the fact that, like the Stratovac II, it was sold mainly through department stores and hardware chains, where markups were too large to permit it a significant price advantage over the more expensive core product. Handivac sold for $79, while the Stratovac II sold for $99. Handivac managers tried to cut costs by going to an overseas supplier for a lighter weight, somewhat less powerful motor – over the vehement objections of Stratovac II designers, who had depended on Handivac's participation in their motor plant to keep their own costs in line.

Eventually, Handivac introduced a cost-reduced "Handivac 403," which sold for $69, importing a 3.0 horsepower motor and cord subassembly from Japan. The enhanced "405" sold for $83. Handivac engineers began at this time to interact with Japanese manufacturing managers. But there were still no distribution channels where Handivac could enjoy the "price busting" opportunity it needed. The most promising channel, though hardly dominant, was the growing chains of catalog stores, which sold the Handivac 403 for $63, a 10% reduction in the department store price.

The Third Generation

During 1976 and 1977, a number of external and internal pressures led to a redesign of the entire product line. Department stores were still the major source of revenue, but competitors were proliferating and the Stratovac II group felt the need to offer an increasing number of more enhanced and more customized products to maintain demand at the profitable high end. Consumers would pay a premium, marketing people believed, only if the company could produce so many versions that all customers felt they were getting the right color with the right options. Moreover, Coolidge had canvassed Stratovac II customers, who hadn't appreciated the "jet sound," as designers had assumed. Bulk was also a problem, as was the vacuum's unattractive look.

Inside the company, Coolidge's two design teams had become more cooperative, particularly as the advantages of molded plastic became obvious to everyone. The hybrid Stratovac II, which had been redesigned in plastic wherever possible, was something of a victory for the young Handivac designers over the more traditional group. Flexibility and cost were the keys to satisfying many markets, and plastics answered both needs. Eventually the more traditional designers also came to see the advantage of going to Japan for a smaller, lighter, more reliable motor – and for a number of subassemblies critical to the company's goal of offering arrays of options.

Concurrently in the mid-1970s, the Handivac designers were pressing for a complete merging of the design engineering teams and for studying Japanese manufacturing techniques. They argued that if flexibility, cost, and quality were going to be crucial, the manufacturing people would have to become more involved in product design. The young guard also believed that Coolidge could produce motors domestically – at required levels of quality – if it adopted certain innovations in machine tool and winding automation and instituted statistical process control at its existing motor plant.

Where the younger design group still lacked credibility, however, was on the bottom line. Top management was reluctant to give up on a two-track approach when the Handivac group had failed to deliver an appliance that made even as much as the Housekeeper line. The number of catalog stores was growing, and newer discount appliance chains were springing up in big cities, but the Handivac faced intense competition. Could the younger designers hope to come in with enough products, offering enough features, and at low enough costs to meet this competition?

Do your designers really understand what manufacturing can deliver?

In the end, Coolidge management decided to develop two core product families in its third generation (see the gatefold). The Stratovac II team redesigned the high-end vacuum cleaner in six models, the "Challenger 6000" series. All appliances in this series came with a power head and a new bag system. By steps – 6001, 6002, and upward – consumers could buy increasingly sophisticated electronic controls. And they could order the 6004 and 6005 in an array of colors.

The 6000 series was constructed almost entirely of molded plastic. Manufacturing came up with an automated way of applying hot sealant to critical seams, and the Challenger's motor was quieter.

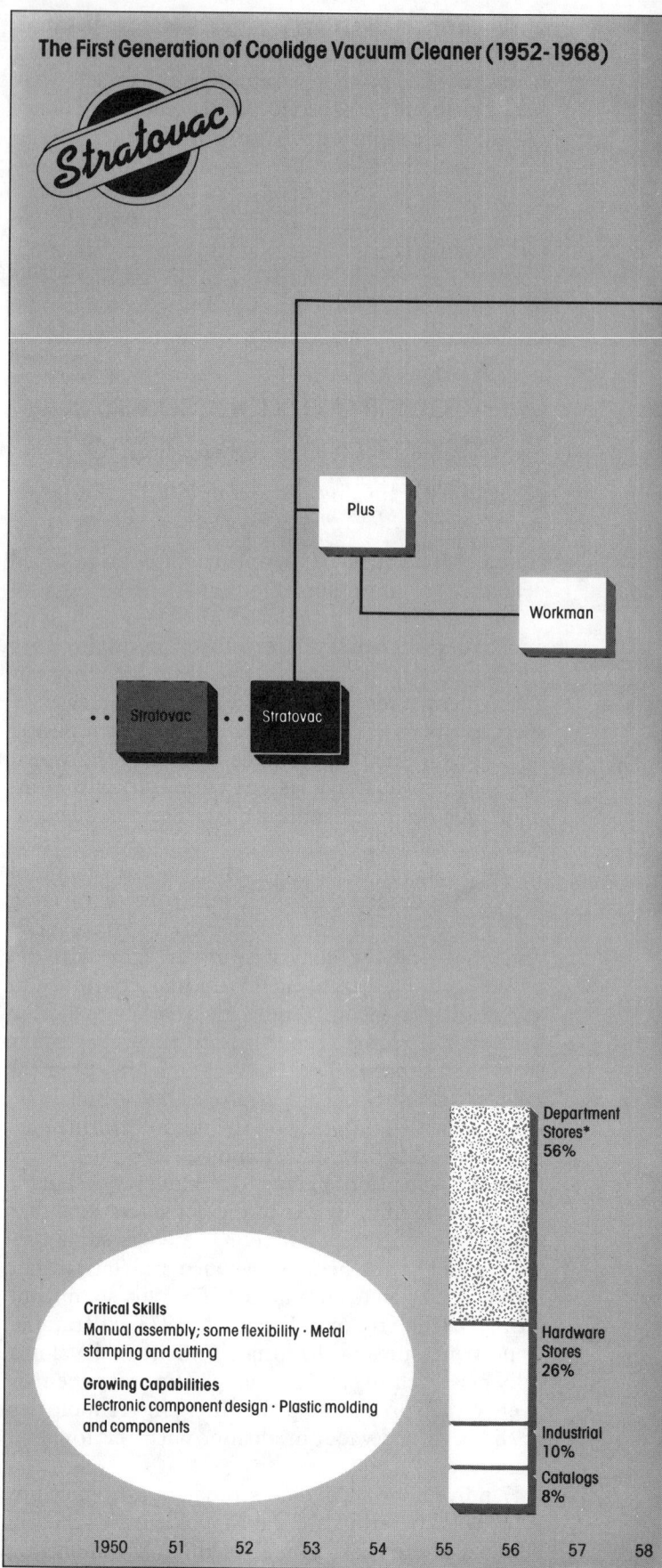

The new product development map 21

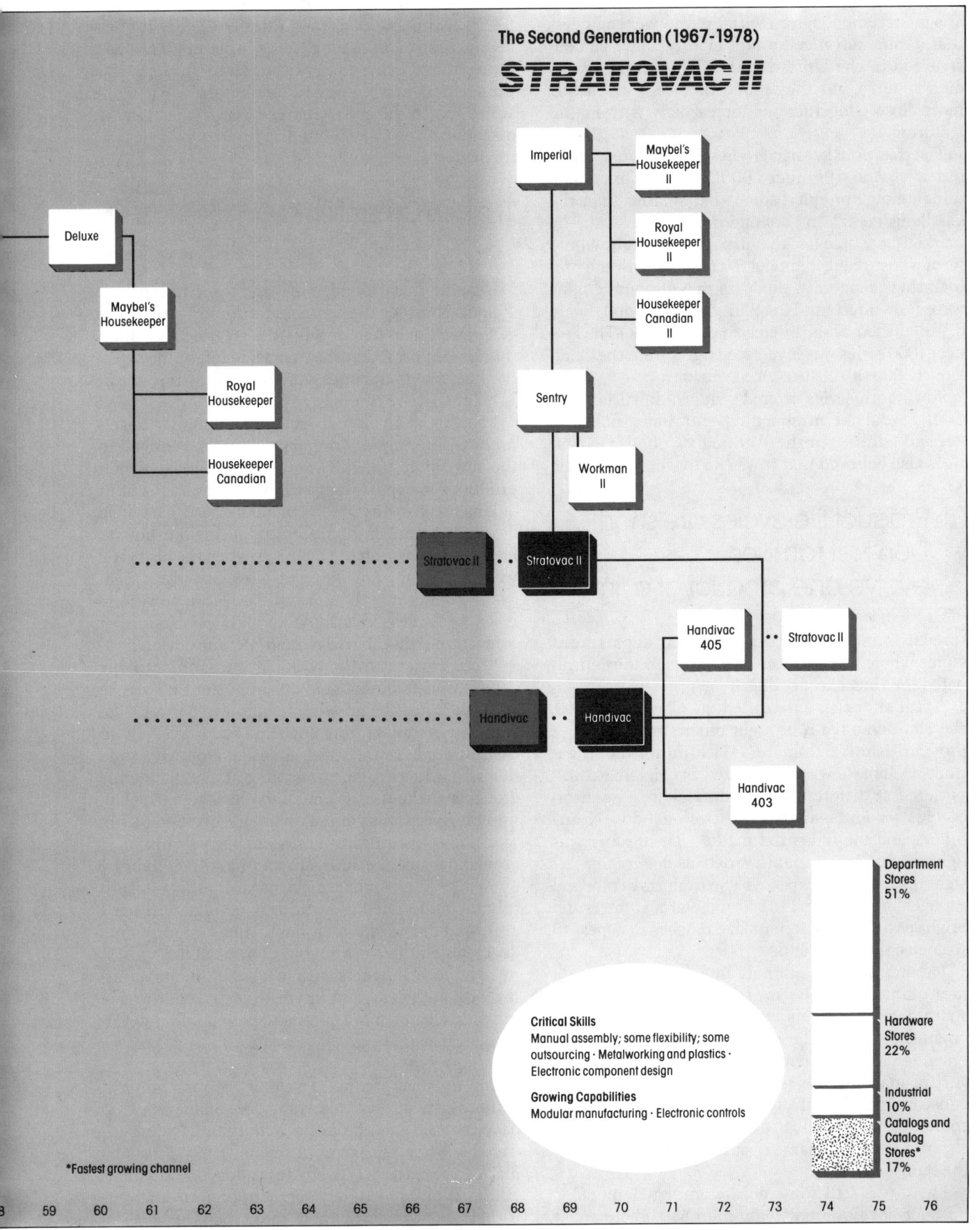

Top management agreed with the younger engineers that a more advanced motor factory could be constructed in the United States. The design teams didn't merge, but they found themselves working more closely together and increasingly with manufacturing.

The traditional design group simultaneously came out with the "Pioneer 4000" series. This was a middle-range product, somewhat smaller than the Challenger 6000, and not offering a power head. The marketing people felt that department stores would want a cost-reduced model to compete with the proliferating "economy" products that discount chains were now offering. (The 4001, 4002, and 4003 were distinguished, again, by electronic controls.) The Pioneer 4000 series was leveraged largely from the Challenger 6000 as a cost-reduced version.

Since both series offered stripped-down models, Coolidge did not introduce a specific industrial product and eliminated the Workman. Coolidge executives also believed that it was no longer worthwhile

> **Product life cycles are short. Don't let families evolve one product at a time.**

to customize models for particular department stores where margins were shrinking, so they eliminated the Housekeeper line.

A year after they introduced the Challenger 6000, the Handivac team brought out its new series of products, the "Helpmate." With minor modifications, Helpmate was customized as "Helpmate SE," targeted at different low-end market segments—college students, apartment dwellers, do-it-yourselfers, and the industrial market. The cleaner was lightweight. Attachments varied, as did graphic design: the company expected a Spartan gray color and a longer hose to appeal to commercial customers and bright pastels and different size brushes to appeal to women college students.

The key to the Helpmate line, however, was its manufacturing. The motor was no longer outsourced, and designers worked with manufacturing engineers on modular components and subassemblies. Top management agreed to set aside manufacturing space in the assembly plants for cellular construction of the Helpmate so that the company could respond quickly to demand for particular models. And Helpmate came in at two-thirds the price of the Pioneer 4000.

There was still some debate among Helpmate's product development team members about most likely channels. Some saw it designed only for discount chains and catalog stores, which by 1978 had pretty much eclipsed hardware stores. Others saw the Helpmate as a low-end product for department stores too. In the end, Helpmate was a smash in the discount stores and all but disappeared from department stores.

The Next Generation?

Imagine that Coolidge managers are gathered in 1985 to consider the company's future. Their three-generation map has simplified a great deal of information—information the managers might intuitively understand but could not have looked at so clearly before. Where can they go from here?

Looking at their map, it's clear that Coolidge's product offerings are not appropriately matched to the new environment. They have aimed most of their products at department stores, and now discount chains are growing at a tremendous rate. They had devoted too much attention to figuring out how to leverage products at the high end, when the big battle was shaping up at the low end. Now Coolidge's managers wonder how long it will be before power options and accessories show up on cheaper, sturdier import lines distributed to high-volume outlets.

More growth in the company's manufacturing capabilities is obviously very important now. The map indicates the growing reciprocity between design and manufacturing engineers, owing largely to the initiatives of the younger design group. It would not be hard to imagine a merging of all engineering groups and the use of temporary dedicated development teams at this point. Product life cycles have obviously been shrinking; designers have to think fast now and cooperate across functional lines. To bring out a new line of inexpensive products that are both reliable and varied in options, Coolidge will need automated, flexible manufacturing systems. This development means bringing all parts of the company together—designers with marketing, manufacturing with both. It means, interestingly enough, a need for even clearer, more complete new product development maps.

The finished product development map presented here may appear elementary, but managers who have mapped their products' evolution have experienced substantial payoff in several areas. First, the map can be extremely useful to product development efforts. It helps focus development projects and limit their scope, making them more manageable. The map helps set specifications and targets for individual projects, provides a context for relating concurrent projects to one another, and indicates how the sequence of projects capitalizes on the company's previous investments. These benefits do much to minimize the likelihood of encountering two of the pitfalls we identified at the outset of this article, the moving target and the lack of product distinctiveness.

A second important benefit is the motivation the map provides the various functional groups – all with a stake in effective product development – to develop their own complementary strategies. As illustrated in the Coolidge Corporation example, the product development map raises a number of issues regarding distribution channels, product technology, and manufacturing approaches that must be answered in all parts of the company if the map is to represent the organization's agreed-on direction.

This point brings up the need for "submaps" in each functional area. In the Coolidge case, the first couple of product generations may not have shown the need for a more careful distribution channel map, but by the third the need is painfully clear. Capturing other strategic marketing variables in, say, a price map, a competitive product positioning map, and a customer map would enable the marketing function to identify and present important trends in the marketplace, define targets for future product offerings, and provide guidance for developing and committing sales and marketing resources.

Equally apparent by the third generation is the need for supporting maps in design engineering. A set of design engineering submaps can produce a clearer sense of the mix of engineering talent the company requires, how it should be organized and focused, and the rate at which the company should bring new technologies into future product generations. These maps would not only help managers integrate design resources with product development efforts but would also ensure that they hire and train new employees in a timely and effective manner and that they focus new project tools (such as computer-aided engineering) on pressing product development needs. The key is achieving technical agreement in advance of product development.

Toward the end of the third generation at Coolidge, the map reveals the need for more detailed manufacturing functional maps to bring out issues raised in the "critical skills" oval. Such maps would focus on strategic issues relating to manufacturing facilities, vendor relationships, and automation technology.

Again, the development of such functional submaps not only benefits manufacturing but also helps the company maximize the return on new product development resources. The most interesting and useful benefits will come out of debates about what to put in the submaps.

Submaps capture the essence of the functional strategies, and when integrated with the new product development map, serve to tie those functional strategies together and provide both a foundation and a process for achieving a company's business strategy. The whole process facilitates the cross-functional discussion and resolution of strategic issues. How often have well-intentioned functional managers

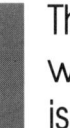

> **The map shows what the product line is not doing.**

met to discuss their various substrategies only to have those from other functions tune out within the first two minutes, as the discussion becomes too technical, too detailed, or simply too parochial to comprehend?

Mapping provides a process for planning that avoids too much detail (like budgeting) and too much parochialism (like traditional functional strategy sessions). Managers will inevitably develop linkages across the organization by going through the steps of selecting the resources or factors to develop into a map, identifying the key dimensions to capture in the map, reviewing historical data to understand the relationships of those dimensions, and examining what is likely to drive future versions of the map. Functions can share their maps to communicate, refine, and agree on important product strategy choices. It is the sharing of functional capabilities – capabilities applied in a systematic, repetitive fashion to product development opportunities – that will become the company's competitive advantage.

Reprint 89315

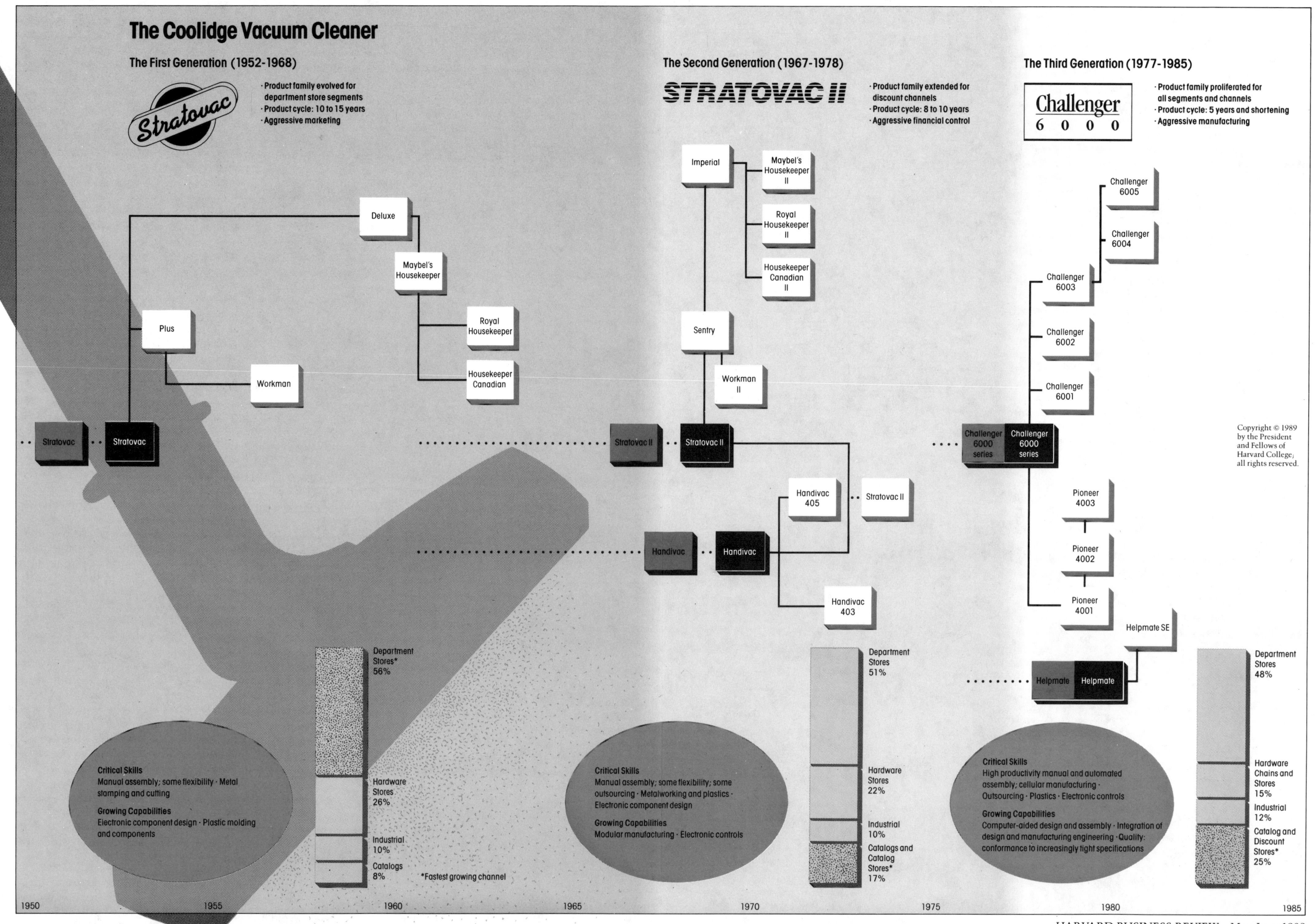

GETTING THINGS DONE

Four Steps to Forecast Total Market Demand

Without a total-demand forecast, you're operating in the dark.

by F. WILLIAM BARNETT

Recent history is filled with stories of companies and sometimes even entire industries that have made grave strategic errors because of inaccurate industrywide demand forecasts. For example:
- In 1974, U.S. electric utilities made plans to double generating capacity by the mid-1980s based on forecasts of a 7% annual growth in demand. Such forecasts are crucial since companies must begin building new generating plants five to ten years before they are to come on line. But during the 1975-1985 period, load actually grew at only a 2% rate. Despite the postponement or cancellation of many projects, the excess generating capacity has hurt the industry financial situation and led to higher customer rates.
- The petroleum industry invested $500 billion worldwide in 1980 and 1981 because it expected oil prices to rise 50% by 1985. The estimate was based on forecasts that the market would grow from 52 million barrels of oil a day in 1979 to 60 million barrels in 1985. Instead, demand had fallen to 46 million barrels by 1985. Prices collapsed, creating huge losses in drilling, production, refining, and shipping investments.
- In 1983 and 1984, 67 new types of business personal computers were introduced to the U.S. market, and most companies were expecting explosive growth. One industry forecasting service projected an installed base of 27 million units by 1988; another predicted 28 million units by 1987. In fact, only 15 million units had been shipped by 1986. By then, many manufacturers had abandoned the PC market or gone out of business altogether.

The inaccurate suppositions did not stem from a lack of forecasting techniques; regression analysis, historical trend smoothing, and others were available to all the players. Instead, they shared a mistaken fundamental assumption: that relationships driving demand in the past would continue unaltered. The companies didn't foresee changes in end-user behavior or understand their market's saturation point. None realized that history can be an unreliable guide as domestic economies become more international, new technologies emerge, and industries evolve.

As a result of changes like these, many managers have come to distrust traditional techniques. Some even throw up their hands and assume that business planning must proceed without good demand forecasts. I disagree. It is possible to develop valuable insights into future market conditions and demand levels based on a deep understanding of the forces behind total-market demand. These insights can sometimes make the difference between a winning strategy and one that flounders.

A forecast of total-market demand won't guarantee a successful strategy. But without it, decisions on investment, marketing support, and other resource allocations will be based on hidden, unconscious assumptions about industrywide requirements, and they'll often be wrong. By gauging total-market demand explicitly, you have a better chance of controlling your company's destiny. Merely going through the process has merit for a management team. Instead of just coming out with pat answers, numbers, and targets, the team is forced to rethink the competitive environment.

Total-market forecasting is only the first stage in creating a strategy. When you've finished your forecast, you're not done with the planning process by any means.

There are four steps in any total-market forecast:
1. Define the market.
2. Divide total industry demand into its main components.
3. Forecast the drivers of demand in each segment and project how they are likely to change.
4. Conduct sensitivity analyses to understand the most critical assumptions and to gauge risks to the baseline forecast.

Defining the market

At the outset, it's best to be overly inclusive in defining the total market. Define it broadly enough to include *all* potential end users so that you can both identify the appropriate drivers of demand and reduce

Bill Barnett is a principal in the Atlanta office of McKinsey & Company. He is a leader of the firm's Microeconomics Center, and his client work has focused on business unit and corporate strategy.

the risk of surprise product substitutions.

The factors that drive forecasts of total-market size differ markedly from those that determine a particular product's market share or product-category share. For example, total-market demand for office telecommunications products nationally depends in part on the number of people in offices and their needs and habits, while total demand for PBX systems depends on how they compare on price and benefits with substitute products like the local telephone company's central office switching service. Beyond this, demand for a particular PBX is a function of price and benefit comparisons with other PBXs.

In defining the market, an understanding of product substitution is critical. Customers might behave differently if the price or performance of potential substitute products changes. One company studying total demand for industrial paper tubes had to consider closely related uses of metal and plastic tubes to prevent customer switching among tubes from biasing the results.

Understand, too, that a completely new product could displace one that hitherto had comprised the entire market—like the electronic calculator, which eliminated the slide rule. For a while after AT&T's divestiture, the Bell telephone companies continued to forecast volume of long-distance calls by using historical trend lines of their revenues—as if they were still part of a monopoly. Naturally, these forecasts grew more inaccurate with time as end users were presented with new choices. The companies are now broadening their market definitions to take account of heightened competition from other long-distance carriers.

There are several ways you can make sure you include all important substitute products (both current and potential). From interviews with industrial customers you can learn about substitutes they are studying or about product usage patterns that imply future switching opportunities. Moreover, market research can lead to insights about consumer products. Speaking with experts in the relevant technologies or reviewing technological literature can help you identify potential developments that could threaten your industry.

Finally, careful quantification of the economic value of alternative products to different customers can yield deep insights into potential switching behavior—for example, how oil price movements would affect plastics prices, which in turn would affect plastic products' ability to substitute for metal or paper.

Analyses like these can lead to the construction of industry demand curves—graphs representing the relationship between price and volume. With an appropriate definition, the total-industry demand curves will often be steeper than demand curves for individual products in the industry. Consumers, for example, are far more likely to switch from Maxwell House to Folgers coffee if Maxwell House's prices increase than they are to stop buying coffee if all coffee prices rise.

In some cases, managers can make quick judgments about market definition. In other cases, they'll have to give their market considerable thought and analysis. A total-market forecast may not be critical to business strategy if market definition is very difficult or the products under study have small market shares. Instead, your principal challenge may be to understand product substitution and competitiveness. One company analyzed the potential market for new consumer food cans, and it concluded that growth trends in food product markets were not critical to the strategy question. What was critical was knowing the value positions of the new packages relative to metal cans, glass jars, and composite cans. So the company spent time on that subject.

Dividing demand into component parts

The second step in forecasting is to divide total demand into its main components for separate analysis.

There are two criteria to keep in mind when choosing segments: make each category small and homogeneous enough so that the drivers of demand will apply consistently across its various elements; make each large enough so that the analysis will be worth the effort. Of course, this is a matter of judgment.

You may find it useful in making this judgment to imagine alternative segmentations (based on end-use customer groups, for example, or type of purchase). Then hypothesize their key drivers of demand (discussed later) and decide how much detail is required to capture the true

> **Americans bought half as many computers as the industry had predicted.**

situation. As the assessment continues, managers can return to this stage and reexamine whether the initial decisions still stand up.

Managers may wish to use a "tree" diagram like the accompanying one constructed by a management team in 1985 to study demand for paper. In this disguised example, industry data permitted the division of demand into 12 end-use categories. Some categories, like business forms and reprographic paper, were big contributors to total consumption; others, such as labels, were not. One (other converting) was fairly large but too diverse for deep analysis. The team focused on the four segments that accounted for 80% of 1985 demand. It then developed secondary branches of the tree to further dissect these categories and to determine their drivers of demand. It analyzed the remaining segments less completely (that is, via a regression against broad macroeconomic trends).

Other companies have used similar methods to segment total demand. One company divided demand for maritime satellite terminals by type of ship (e.g., seismic ships, bulk/cargo/container ships). Another divided demand for long-distance telephone service into business and residential customers

Four steps to forecast total market demand 31

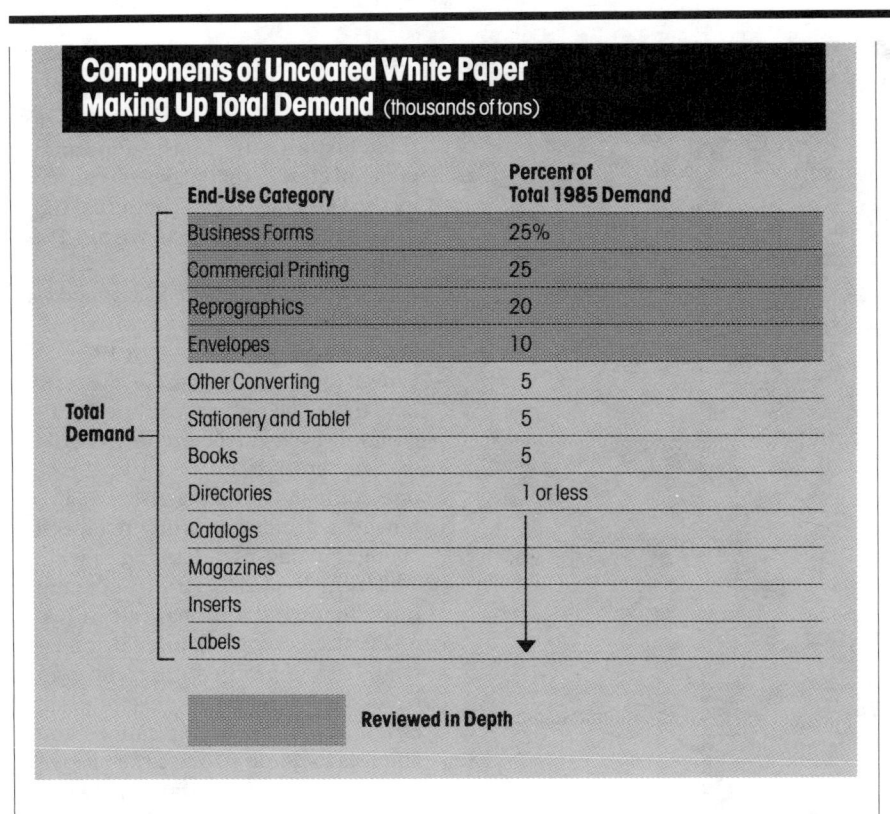

Components of Uncoated White Paper Making Up Total Demand (thousands of tons)

Total Demand
End-Use Category	Percent of Total 1985 Demand
Business Forms	25%
Commercial Printing	25
Reprographics	20
Envelopes	10
Other Converting	5
Stationery and Tablet	5
Books	5
Directories	1 or less
Catalogs	
Magazines	
Inserts	
Labels	

▮ Reviewed in Depth

and then subdivided it by usage level. And a third segmented consumer appliances into three purchase types—appliances used in new home construction, replacement appliance sales in existing homes, and appliance penetration in existing homes.

In thinking about market divisions, managers need to decide whether to use existing data on segment sizes or to commission research to get an independent estimate. Reliable public information on historical demand levels by segment is available for many big U.S. industries (like steel, automobiles, and natural gas) from industry associations, the federal government, off-the-shelf studies by industry experts, or ongoing market data services. For some foreign markets and less well-researched industries in the United States, like the labels industry, you may have to get independent estimates. Even with good data sources, however, the readily available information may not be divided into the best categories to support an insightful analysis. In these cases, managers must decide whether to develop their forecasts based on the available historical data or to undertake their own market research programs, which can be time-consuming and expensive.

Note that while such segmentation is sufficient for forecasting total demand, it may not create categories useful for developing a marketing strategy. A single product may be driven by entirely different factors. One study of industrial components found that consumer industry categories provided a good basis for projecting total-market demand but gave only limited help in formulating a strategy based on customer preferences: distinguishing those who buy on price from those who buy on service, product quality, or other benefits. Such buying-factor categories generally do not correlate with the customer industry categories used for forecasting. A strong sales force, however, can identify customer preferences and develop appropriate account tactics for each one.

Forecasting the drivers of demand

The third step is to understand and forecast the drivers of demand in each category. Here you can make good use of regressions and other statistical techniques to find some causes for changes in historical demand. But this is only a start. The tougher challenge is to look beyond the data on which regressions can easily be based to other factors where data are much harder to find. Then you need to develop a point of view on how those other factors may themselves change in the future.

An end-use analysis from the commodity paper example, reprographic paper, is shown in the accompanying chart. The management team, using available data, divided reprographic paper into two categories: plain-paper copier paper and nonimpact page printer paper. Without this important differentiation, the drivers of demand would have been masked, making it hard to forecast effectively.

In most cases, managers can safely assume that demand is affected both by macroeconomic variables and by industry-specific developments. In looking at plain-paper copier paper, the team used simple and multiple regression analyses to test relationships with macroeconomic factors like white-collar workers, population, and economic performance. Most of the factors had a significant effect on demand. Intuitively, it also made sense to the team that the level of business activity would relate to paper consumption levels. (Economists sometimes refer to growth in demand due to factors like these as an "outward shift" in the demand curve—toward a greater quantity demanded at a given price.)

Demand growth for copy paper, however, had exceeded the real rate of economic growth and the challenge was to find what other factors had been causing this. The team hypothesized that declining copy costs had caused this increased usage. The relationship was proved by estimating the substantial cost reductions that had occurred, combining those with numbers of tons produced over time, and then fashioning an indicative demand curve for copy paper. (See the chart "Understanding Copy Paper Demand Drivers.") The clear relationship between cost and volume meant that cost

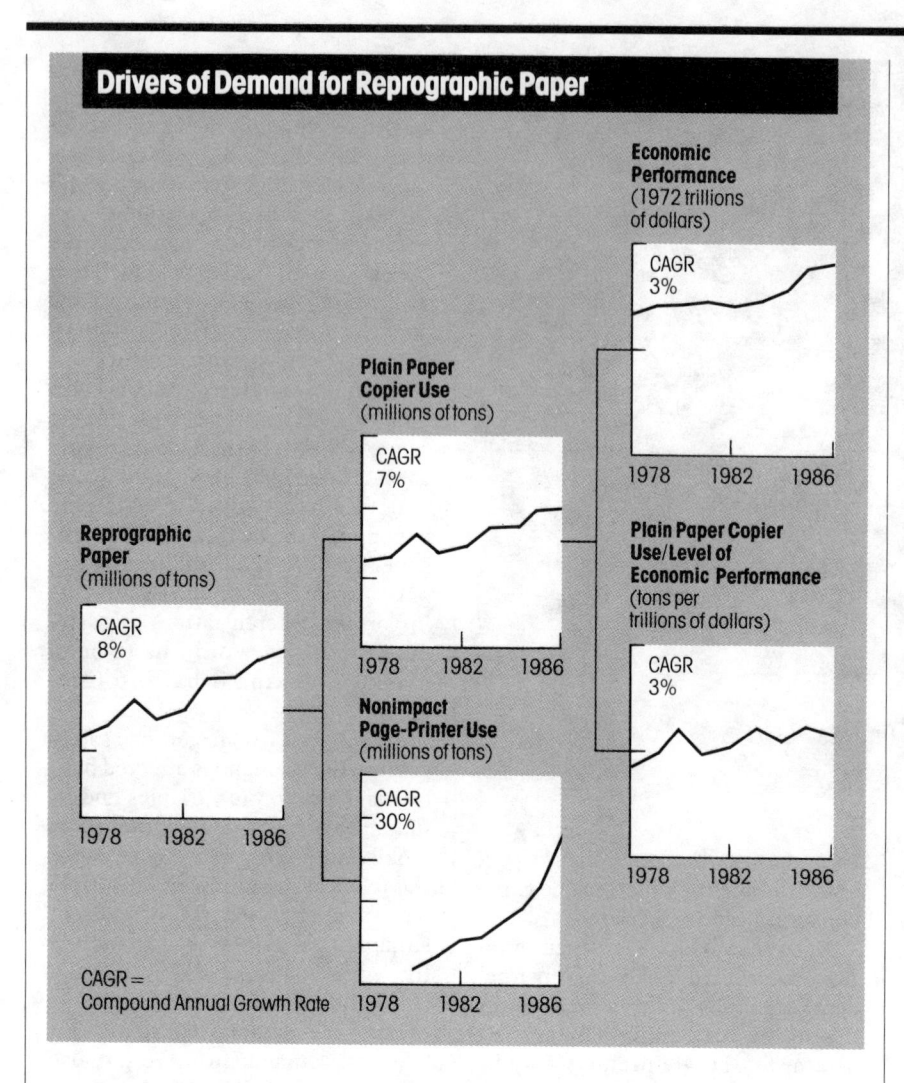

Drivers of Demand for Reprographic Paper

Reprographic Paper (millions of tons) — CAGR 8% (1978–1986)

Plain Paper Copier Use (millions of tons) — CAGR 7% (1978–1986)

Nonimpact Page-Printer Use (millions of tons) — CAGR 30% (1978–1986)

Economic Performance (1972 trillions of dollars) — CAGR 3% (1978–1986)

Plain Paper Copier Use/Level of Economic Performance (tons per trillions of dollars) — CAGR 3% (1978–1986)

CAGR = Compound Annual Growth Rate

---

reductions had been an important cause of past demand growth. (Economists sometimes describe this as a downward-shifting supply curve leading to movement down the demand curve.)

Further major declines in cost per copy seemed unlikely because paper costs were expected to remain flat, and the data indicated little increase in price elasticity, even if cost per copy fell further. So the team concluded that usage growth (per level of economic performance) was likely to continue the flattening trend begun in 1983: growth in copy paper consumption would be largely a function of economic growth, not cost declines as in the past. The team then reviewed several econometric services forecasts to develop a base case economic forecast.

Similar studies have been performed in other industries. A simple one was the industrial components analysis mentioned before, a case where the total forecast was used as background but was not critical to the company's strategy decision. Here the team divided demand into its consuming industries and then asked experts in each industry for production forecasts. Total demand for components was projected on the assumption that it would move parallel to a weight-averaged forecast of these customer industries. Actual demand three years later was 2% above the team's prediction, probably because the industry experts underestimated the impact of the economic recovery of 1984 and 1985.

In another example, a team forecasting demand for maritime satellite terminals extrapolated past penetration curves for each of five categories of ships. These curves were then adjusted for major changes in the shipping industry (e.g., adding the depressing effect of the growing oil glut, taking out of these historical trends the unnatural demand growth that had been caused by the Falklands war). The actual figure three years later was within 1% of the forecast.

Knowing the drivers of demand is crucial to the success of any total-market demand forecast. In 1974, as I mentioned earlier, most electric utilities used an incomplete total-demand forecast to predict robust demand growth. In the early 1980s, one company's management team, however, decided to study potential changes in end-user demand as well. The team divided electricity demand into the three traditional categories: residential, commercial, and industrial. It then profiled differences in residential demand because of more efficiency in home appliances and changes in home size and the ratio of multi-unit to single-family dwellings. Industrial demand was analyzed by evaluating the future of several key consuming industries, paying special attention to changes in their total production and electricity use. This end-use approach sharply reduced the utility's initial forecasts and led to cancellation of two $700 million generating plants then in the planning stage.

In 1983, forecasters in the U.S. personal computer industry were saying that demand would continue to rise at a rapid rate because there were 50 million white-collar workers and only 8 million installed PCs. One company, however, did a more detailed demand forecast that showed that growth would soon flatten out. It found that more than two-thirds of white-collar workers either did not require PCs in their jobs—actors and elevator operators, for instance—or were supported mostly by inexpensive terminals linked to large computers, as in the case of many clerical workers. The potential market was not big enough to support the growth rate. Indeed, the market began to flatten the next year.

Forecasting total demand became crucial for another company that was thinking about acquiring a maker of video games. Many thought

Understanding Copy Paper Demand Drivers

Copy Cost Comparison: 1972 Dollars

(Bar chart: 1975 Total Cost = 10 cents per copy, composed of 1 Cost of Paper and 9 other costs; 1985 Total Cost = 2 cents per copy with Reduced Paper Cost, Savings in Clerical Time, Reduced Consumables' Cost (e.g., Toner), and Savings in Equipment Depreciation accounting for the reduction.)

Copy Paper Demand

Cents per Copy vs. Tons per Billions of Dollars Real GNP (scatter plot with declining trend line)

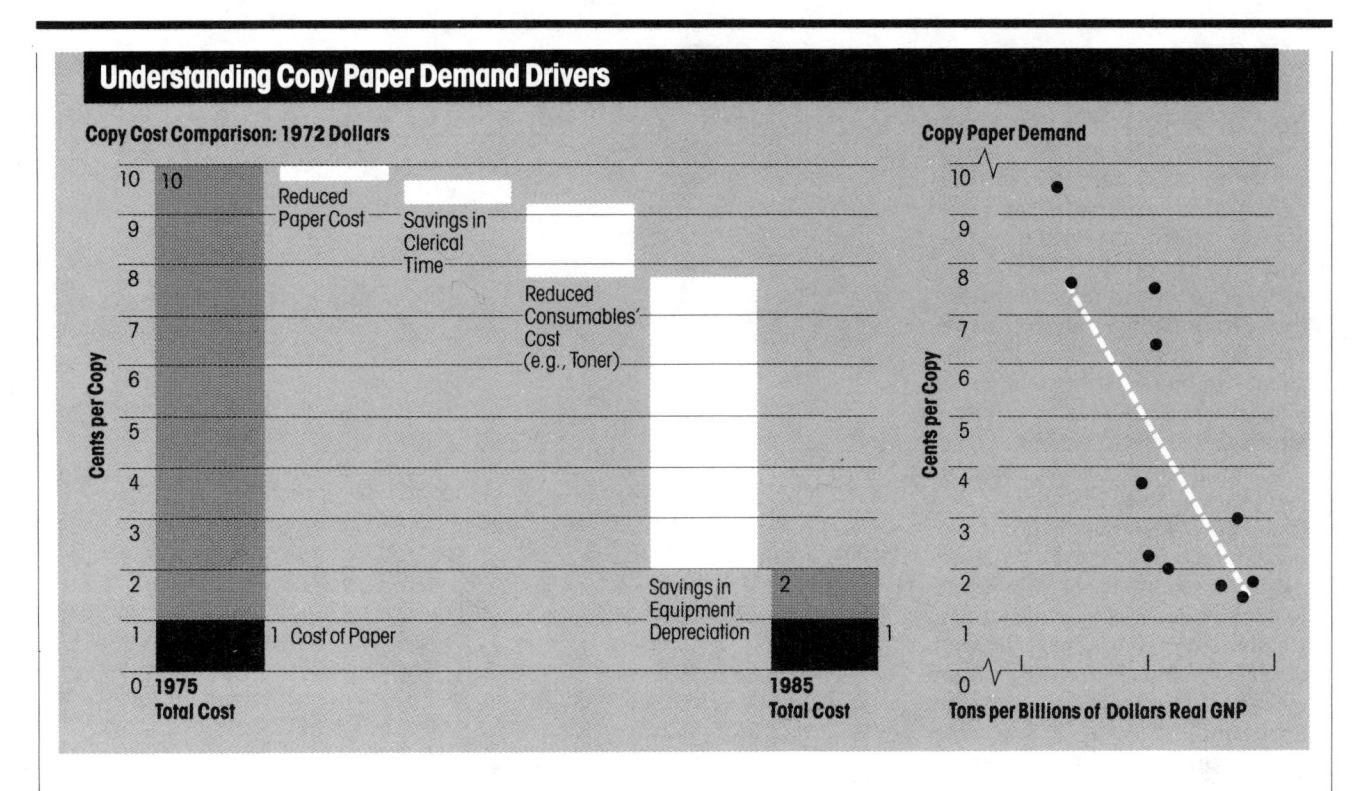

that low overall market penetration (10% of U.S. households) signified a lot of room for growth before the market became saturated, when about 50% of the households would have games. Using available data, however, the management team created categories based on family income and children's ages. The analysis made clear that the main target market, upper-income families with children, was already well penetrated. Families with incomes exceeding $50,000 and children between the ages of 6 and 15 already were 75% penetrated. This finding convinced management that demand would fall and that the proposed acquisition did not make sense. The dramatic decline in video game sales shortly thereafter confirmed the wisdom of this judgment.

Conducting sensitivity analyses

Managers who rely on single-point demand forecasts run dangerous risks. Some of the macroeconomic variables behind the forecasts could be wrong. Despite the best analysis, moreover, the assumptions behind the other demand drivers could also be wrong, especially if discontinuities loom on the horizon. Imaginative marketers who ask questions like "What things could cause this forecast to change dramatically?" produce the best estimates. They are more likely to identify potential risks and discontinuities – developments in competing technologies, in customer industry competitiveness, in supplier cost structures – than those who do not. So once a baseline forecast is complete, the challenge is to determine how far it could be off target.

At one level, such a sensitivity analysis can be done by simply varying assumptions and quantifying their impact on demand. But a more targeted approach usually provides better insight.

Begin such an analysis by thinking through and quantifying the areas of greatest strategic risk. One company's strategy decision may be affected only if demand is well below the baseline forecast; in another case, big risks may result from small forecasting errors.

Next, gauge the likelihood of such a development. In the white paper example, the baseline forecast called for continued market growth, though below historical levels. In any particular year, demand could fluctuate with the economy, but the critical question was whether demand would at some point begin a long decline. If so, the companion supply-curve analysis indicated that prices would probably fall dramatically.

The team created two scenarios of a gradual decline, one based largely on changes in the economy and the other on changes in assumed end-use trends. These scenarios showed what would make demand fall (e.g., different rates of decline in copier prices) and thereby provided a basis for evaluating the likelihood of a downturn.

Determining an appropriate effort

The forecasting framework outlined above can work for both comprehensive and simple assessments, but there are different ways to carry out these analyses. A big challenge in demand forecasting (just as with other types of market analysis) is to gauge the appropriate effort for the project's purpose. It's useful to ask: "How much do I need to know to make the decision at hand?"

Managers can invest a lot of time in such analyses – the paper example took about 8 man-weeks and the large-scale electricity forecast about 14 man-weeks. Some companies have forecasting departments who work year-round on these subjects. The more thorough, though time-consuming, approach generates greater confidence, and the effort will be appropriate where the demand projection can significantly influence corporate strategy (whether to make a several hundred million dollar capital investment, for example), or where there is great uncertainty about total demand.

Often, however, the issues are not complicated, time is limited, or the total demand forecast is not important enough to merit that commitment (for example, the company is looking to add a couple of points to its small market share). In such cases, managers should proceed quickly and inexpensively. They can, for example, rely on experts' judgment or unsophisticated regressions to forecast drivers of demand. Even the limited approaches can yield insights. Furthermore, beginning the demand analysis process can help managers determine whether important demand issues exist that should be analyzed in greater depth.

Total-demand forecasting can be important to strategy decisions. Developing independent forecasts through the four-step framework I've outlined will not only lead to better recommendations but also help build conviction and consensus for action by creating understanding of the drivers of demand and the risks in forecasts.

Even when the work is sound, though, uncertainties will remain: discontinuities will still be difficult to predict, especially if they are rooted in momentous political, macroeconomic, or technological changes. But managers who push their thinking through the steps in this framework will have a better chance of finding these discontinuities than those who do not. And those who base their business strategies on a solid knowledge of demand will stand a much greater chance of making wise investments and competing effectively.

Reprint 88401

Keeping Informed

*Leonard M. Lodish and
David J. Reibstein*

New gold mines and minefields in market research

Technology aids offer more precise consumer data than ever before— to marketers who understand the hazards

The practice of marketing is undergoing radical change. Thanks to new data acquisition technologies and advanced methods of data analysis, marketers are increasingly able to isolate the effects of advertising, pricing, promotion, and other marketing elements. Cable television, for example, enables marketers to experiment with advertising approaches, and the scanning of uniform product codes provides quick feedback on optimal pricing of grocery and other products.

The new availability of such a wealth of marketing data and software has certain dangers, though, the authors caution—especially the tendency to confuse cause and effect. The authors advocate an integrated managerial effort to incorporate the new tools into company decision making. Chief among the requirements of such an effort must be the use of marketing science specialists who are equipped to analyze complicated statistics and accurately separate causes from effects.

Messrs. Lodish and Reibstein are professors of marketing at the University of Pennsylvania's Wharton School, where they specialize in marketing modeling. Both are previous HBR authors—Mr. Lodish of "'Vaguely Right' Approach to Sales Force Allocations" (January-February 1974) and Mr. Reibstein (with Paul W. Farris) of "How Prices, Ad Expenditures, and Profits Are Linked" (November-December 1979).

The secret to a successful marketing career has usually been to have a good understanding of what the customer wants and doesn't want. Without this understanding, it is impossible to devise a suitable advertising, pricing, or product strategy.

How one gets the feel for the market has never been fully determined. Is it something a marketer is born with, or is it learned? How does one come by an ability to empathize with the customer? Whatever the answer, this talent is becoming less important as new technology provides the opportunity to obtain data-based insight into the pulse of the market. With this change in data and analysis comes change in practice and skills.

The evolving technologies allow managers to revolutionize the practice of marketing. The usual assumption in buying behavior is that the customer operates as "a black box." But the box is being opened, and competitive pressures will make the new insights hard to ignore.

New technological options

Consumer packaged-goods industries, in particular, have benefited from the availability of new data and analysis methods for assessing markets. Two advances in data collection have been especially important: split-cable technology and uniform-product-code (UPC) scanners.

Split-cable technology. Television that allows different advertisements to appear on the same television program within the same geographic area is called split cable. In communities having split-cable systems, two neighbors separately watching NBC at the same time can see two different commercials that a research firm has chosen for their viewing. The firm intercepts the network feed and inserts certain commercials in the transmission to selected households.

In split-cable systems, household purchases (which brands at what prices) are recorded. Comparing the purchase behavior of households receiving one ad with that of households receiving another allows researchers to assess the more effective effort. By eliminating the impact of extraneous, uncontrollable factors, such a research approach also enables marketing managers to experiment with advertising strategies.

Most advertising field experiments rely on two or more budget levels (determined generally by number of ads shown) or ad copies (themes or executions) in separate test cities. Comparison of the test cities permits attribution of the variations occurring in the test areas to the different advertising implementations.

To find a match of all the characteristics of one community with another is, of course, very difficult. The alternative is to run each experiment in many cities. Aside from driving the costs up, however, each experimental treatment may get different results. This situation can lead to confusion since variations in the results have to be explained, usually by differences in city demographics, competitive environments, and product distribution.

The split-cable approach puts neighbors in different experimental cells, or treatment groups. In a large sample, the experimental cells are indistinguishable except for the ads they get. Consumers shop within the same group of stores, so that the distribution and effect of product displays and promotion on various cells do not vary.

The approach is most commonly used for budgeting decisions. Nestlé and AT&T have tested two budget levels within one community, approximately 100,000 households receiving each experimental ad campaign. Such tests can cost less than $100,000.

Split-cable systems can also be used for copy testing. For example, AT&T had been quite successful with its "Reach Out" campaign but was not content with the amount of long-distance calling of its light users.[1] Through an attitude survey, the company discovered that light users were overestimating the costs of long-distance calls by as much as 50%. In response, AT&T developed its alternative campaign called "Cost of Visit," which emphasized making use of the economy of "offpeak" hours.

To test this campaign as an alternative to the proven Reach Out theme, AT&T chose to conduct a split-cable experiment. Over 15 months, one group of cable TV subscribers received the Reach Out campaign, while the second group in the same community and watching the same television shows saw the Cost of Visit commercials. AT&T obtained records of telephone use from the telephone company's billing system.

The Cost of Visit strategy produced more long-distance calling during experimentation than the Reach Out strategy, especially among light users. The company estimated that the new copy could generate additional revenue of nearly $100 million over a five-year period—at no additional cost to the phone company.

Prior to using such a split-cable system, little was known about how and under what conditions advertising works or about how to test advertising effectiveness. Now, thanks to

---

[1] These results were taken from Alan Kuritsky, Emily Bassman, John D.C. Little, and Alvin J. Silk, "The Development, Testing, and Execution of a New Marketing Strategy at AT&T Long Lines," *Interfaces*, December 1982, p. 22.

Exhibit I UPC-aided optimal pricing for a retail grocer over 16 weeks

Retail price	Average weekly sales of boxes of Minute Rice	Unit contribution at $.69 cost	Actual total contribution at $.69 cost	Unit contribution at $.79 cost	Anticipated total contribution at $.79 cost
$ .89	80	$.20	$16.00	$.10	$ 8.00
.99	66	.30	19.80	.20	13.20
1.09	62	.40	24.80	.30	19.60
1.19	50	.50	25.00	.40	20.00
1.29	41	.60	24.60	.50	20.50

---

the advent of split-cable technology, marketers can assess the impact of advertising on a micromarket basis.

Uniform-product-code scanners. These devices read and register the prices of items as they are checked out in retail outlets. The scanners automatically track inventories, reduce clerical errors, speed checkout procedures, and ease price changes. They also automatically store a wealth of marketing information—prices, for instance, which make it easy to determine price elasticity. Scanner memories store information on coupon use so that marketers can quickly measure the consumer response to using coupons across product categories. Information about shelf space, end-of-aisle displays, use of cooperative advertising, and the like can be retained on these scanners and then measured with respect to impact on sales, item movement, and net contribution.

A growing number of small organizations specializes in analyzing scanner data to recommend optimal pricing levels to retailers. Primarily, these organizations examine historical demand at various pricing levels and determine the prices at which retailers can maximize total contribution at retail stores.

One retail grocer, for example, offered Minute Rice at five different prices over 16 weeks. The average demand levels, shown in *Exhibit I*, ranged from 80 boxes to 41. With current costs of $.69 per box, the store maximized its contribution from this one item by charging $1.19. At this price, the store generated an average weekly contribution of $25.00 on this item. When the grocer offered Minute Rice at a special promotion price of $.89, the sales volume increased from 50 units at $1.19 to 80 boxes per week. The total weekly unit contribution, however, was only $16.00. The lower price, therefore, did not generate sufficient incremental volume and cost the store $9.00 ($25.00 minus $16.00).

There may, of course, be objectives other than maximizing item contributions. What the system provides is an automated means of quickly scanning the thousands of items in a retail store and, at a minimum, determining the optimal price to charge for each item or the cost of the other objectives.

If the cost of Minute Rice increases to $.79 per box, moreover, then the price that maximizes item contribution is no longer $1.19 but $1.29, as shown in *Exhibit I*. Thus, the system automatically detects optimal new prices to correspond with cost increases.

The approaches combined. Other data-collection firms have gone a step further in integrating data from split-cable television and UPC scanners. They ask a large sample of consumers in several geographic areas that are simultaneously served by split-cable television to complete a questionnaire detailing a wide set of demographic and family characteristics. In return for lottery choices and gifts, respondents are given identification cards to use while they shop in cooperating supermarkets and drugstores, and their homes are connected with a split-cable network. The marketers can track who makes which purchases (via

Exhibit II Cumulative test minus control

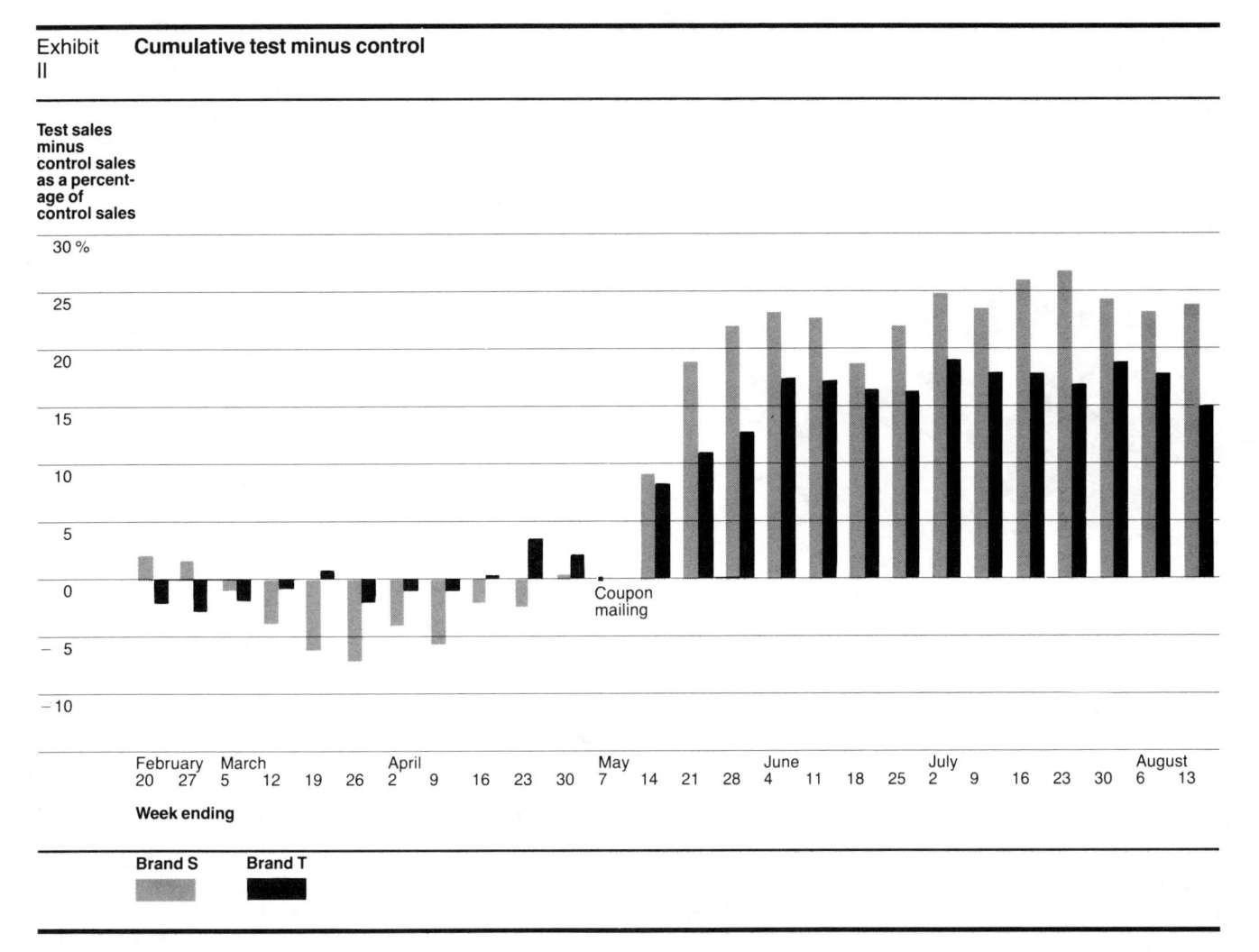

Test sales minus control sales as a percentage of control sales

[Bar chart showing weekly data from February 20 to August 13, with Brand S (gray) and Brand T (black) bars. Values are near zero or slightly negative from February through early May, then rise sharply after "Coupon mailing" in mid-May, reaching roughly 20–27% through June, July, and August.]

Week ending: February 20, 27; March 5, 12, 19, 26; April 2, 9, 16, 23, 30; May 7, 14, 21, 28; June 4, 11, 18, 25; July 2, 9, 16, 23, 30; August 6, 13

Brand S ▨ Brand T ■

the identification numbers) and at which prices, how the products are displayed, whether coupons are used, and which television commercials are shown to which households.

It does not take a brilliant mathematician to use such information to identify how changes in marketing expenditures affect the purchasing behavior of market segments. The wealth of valuable consumer information is almost endless.

Methods & technologies for analysis

Aside from offering exceptional detail, the consumer research techniques of the 1980s have other useful attributes. They allow data to be gathered unobtrusively, to show details about individuals, and to be ready for analysis.

Another major advance is the marketing managers' accessibility to data via computers. No longer are the data relegated to the corporation's data processors. The special marketing-decision software that one can easily learn to use now provides managers a way to combine modeling, statistics, graphics, flexible report generation, and data-base management.

Microanalysis and consumer promotion. A combination of scanner panels, computer technology, and microanalysis is now available to consumer product companies so that they can improve their use of consumer coupons. From 1975 to 1981, the distribution of consumer coupons increased from 36 billion to 102.4 billion.

Most companies look at the redemption rates of coupons as a measure of their success. But what do redemption rates have to do with profit? And what would happen if the companies ran different coupon promotions or if they ran no coupon promotions at all?

There is a syndicated service that mails out coupons to one group in a scanner panel and that tracks a matched control group which receives no coupons. Analysts at the service then compare the sales volumes of the group that has been exposed to the coupons and of the group that has not. *Exhibit II* shows the sales effect of coupons for two different brands. It is quite easy to compare these sales with those of the no-coupon group. Notice how sharply sales rose after the mailing of the coupons.

The figures show only the short-term, obvious sales effects of coupon mailing. To determine the long-term effects, marketers need to apply mathematical models of consumer brand choice and loyalty. Do those who get coupons change their brand loyalty, and does it last? Is the use of a coupon for an established product by somebody who has not tried it

Exhibit III	Bimonthly market shares July-August 1979 – July-August 1981

Abel's share

Unit share

| 5.75 % |
| 5.50 |
| 5.25 |
| 5.00 |
| 4.75 |
| 4.50 |
| 4.25 |
| 4.00 |

July-August 1979 · July-August 1980 · July-August 1981

Baker's share

Unit share

| 5.5 % |
| 5.0 |
| 4.5 |
| 4.0 |
| 3.5 |
| 3.0 |
| 2.5 |
| 2.0 |

July-August 1979 · July-August 1980 · July-August 1981

Cain's share

Unit share

| 5.5 % |
| 5.0 |
| 4.5 |
| 4.0 |
| 3.5 |
| 3.0 |
| 2.5 |
| 2.0 |

July-August 1979 · July-August 1980 · July-August 1981

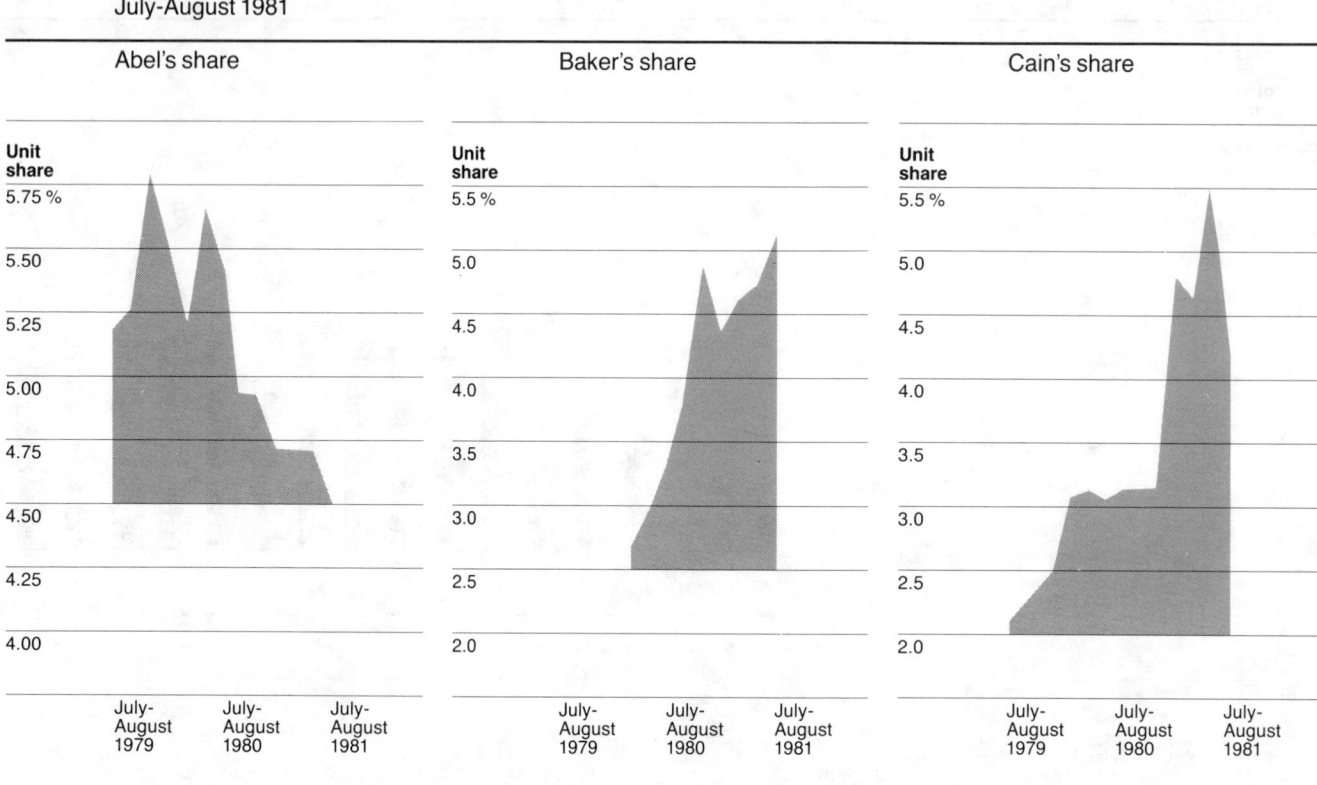

for a while just like a new trial for a new product? These are questions such models are designed to answer.

Microanalysis and consumer choice. The combination of computer technology and the new levels of data refinement (micro levels) have brought about a revolutionary development in marketing decision models. The models forecast choices of product and service purchases. Each choice the consumer makes is modeled as a function of all the variables that may be affecting the customer at that point. These include variables that the manufacturer and retailer control, such as shelf price, advertising, and promotion, as well as uncontrollable behavior like brand loyalty, size loyalty, and price responsiveness.

These micro-level choice models enable marketers to evaluate more decision variables than ever before and to predict more precisely the effect of marketing activities on sales and market share. For example, it used to be difficult to forecast the impact of advertising, promotion, and display variables on the retail market share of Coke and Pepsi. With the aid of a micro-level choice model, a scanner panel, and the appropriate computer technology, marketers can now make highly informed predictions.

No longer do marketing experiments require the manipulation of marketing expenditures in large geographical areas. The use of split-cable television and scanner panels or other micro-level data enables researchers to use much smaller experimental units, such as areas of a city or groups of households. The individual consumer can now be the unit of analysis, and every home the object of observation. Getting statistically significant results with these smaller experimental units is much easier and cheaper than in the recent past.

Dangers on the marketing horizon

Two problems could compromise the potential of the new micro-level experimentation and decision support software. The first is senior management's not putting the costs and benefits of the microexperimentation data into perspective. Even though manipulating marketing variables within these microexperiments costs less than do traditional experiments, the cost of the data is higher. Scanner panels and split-cable data are not cheap – they cost about $150,000 per year per product class per microtest market.

As long as the short-term focus prevalent in American industry dominates most companies, they cannot take advantage of the potential of these micro-level experiments. The reason is simple. The experimental and data-collection costs are usually in a market research budget, which is not considered to belong to the same framework as the budgets for advertising, pricing, promotion, and distribution, all of which market research supports. A $200,000 cost for data seems like a lot of money to put into a market research budget. When one looks at the leverage that advertising, promotion, and the sales force get and the improvement of decisions that comes from such

Exhibit IV — Regional market share changes, Abel and Baker
First half of 1981 in comparison with last half of 1980

Change in Abel's share in share points

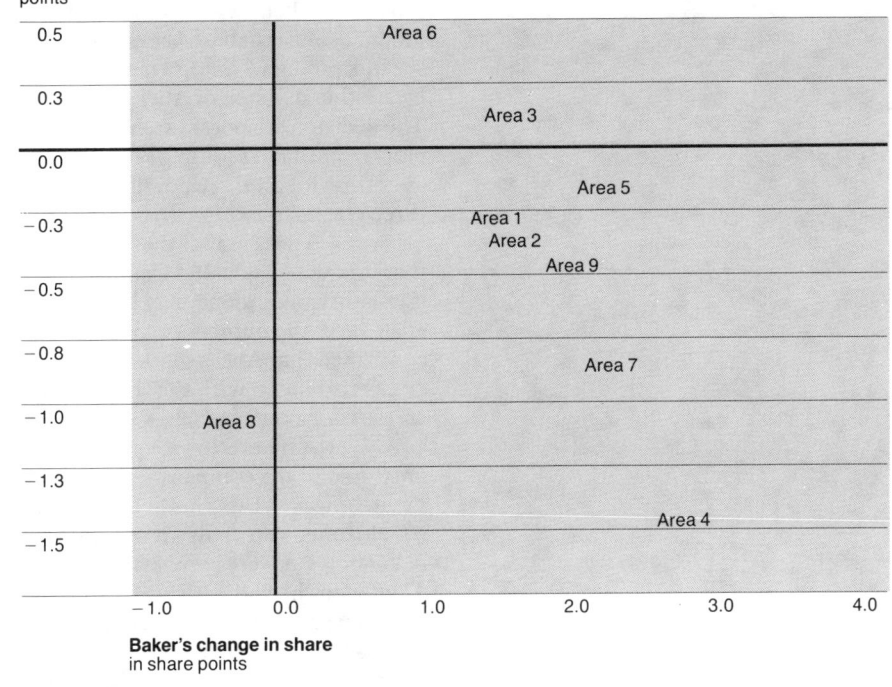

Baker's change in share (share points)	Area
~1.8, 0.5	Area 6
~1.8, 0.3	Area 3
~1.5, -0.3	Area 5
~1.3, -0.3	Area 1
~1.4, -0.4	Area 2
~1.7, -0.5	Area 9
~2.0, -0.8	Area 7
~-0.7, -1.0	Area 8
~2.7, -1.3	Area 4

Baker's change in share in share points

---

data, however, the costs seem inconsequential.

The second problem is management's tendency to interpret results using simple data analysis methods. One has to use the appropriate model and statistical analysis to ensure that the results are indeed real and not statistical artifacts.

How to avoid the pitfalls

We have observed a tendency in marketing (as well as in other areas) to use computers to make employees' jobs easier rather than to enable employees to do their jobs better. Managers have a tendency to favor computers to eliminate clerical labor and automate the tedious parts of management jobs. But the real potential of the new technology lies in improving marketing decisions. Since most of the clerical procedures formerly used to analyze marketing data were fairly simple, managers have gravitated toward very simple computer marketing analyses.

The new technology also has great potential for misuse. For example, there has been a growing use of menu-driven computer systems. These systems have lists of reports that managers may choose from. But such systems limit the complexity of an analysis because they look at data two factors at a time. They use cross-tabulation or various plots of marketing instruments, such as advertising and sales over time. These systems can be wonderful for hypothesis generation or for developing questions that need detailed answers. Without appropriate checks and interpretation by knowledgeable, sophisticated analysts, however, these reports can cause more harm than good.

It is possible to use the new data bases to estimate the degree to which various marketing factors influence sales, but the standard technology to automate complete market response analysis is just not here yet.

There may be other extraneous factors causing sales response. For example, if you take a cross-sectional look at the advertising and sales for a product, you may conclude that the advertising causes the sales. After all, the graph a computer menu produces may show a rise in advertising associated with a rise in sales.

But what this analysis may really be saying is that large cities are bigger than small cities. Obviously, large cities have larger sales and larger advertising budgets than small cities. If population is statistically factored out of the analysis, a very different picture can emerge. Not only is population a factor that should be included, but promotion, distribution, and pricing – of both the product and the competitors in question – also need to be considered simultaneously.

It is difficult to resist a beautiful graph relating advertising and sales in a striking multicolor format. GIGO, "garbage in, garbage out," was a very true description of the data processing that was popular 10 to 15 years ago. Now a new slogan has become popular and is even more true: "Garbage in, *color* garbage out."

The new generation of managers and young people who are no longer afraid of the computer may be a mixed blessing. The most that any market analysis (no matter how sophisticated) can do is decipher what has happened – that is, what worked and what did not work in the past. No system will necessarily predict aspects of the future that are not similar to aspects of the past. Management cannot use the computer as a substitute for rational, creative thinking. Rather, the computer is best used as a support system for strategy formulation.

An example helps illustrate our point. A large retailer with many stores was seeking to determine the best media through which to advertise a new consumer electronics product. Its advertising agency was recommending magazines, while others in the company were recommending newspapers, radio, and television. The company's managers developed a program whereby two cities would receive one experimental ad campaign for three months.

Data for the product accumulated on electronic cash registers, and the experiment's results were available a week after the experiment

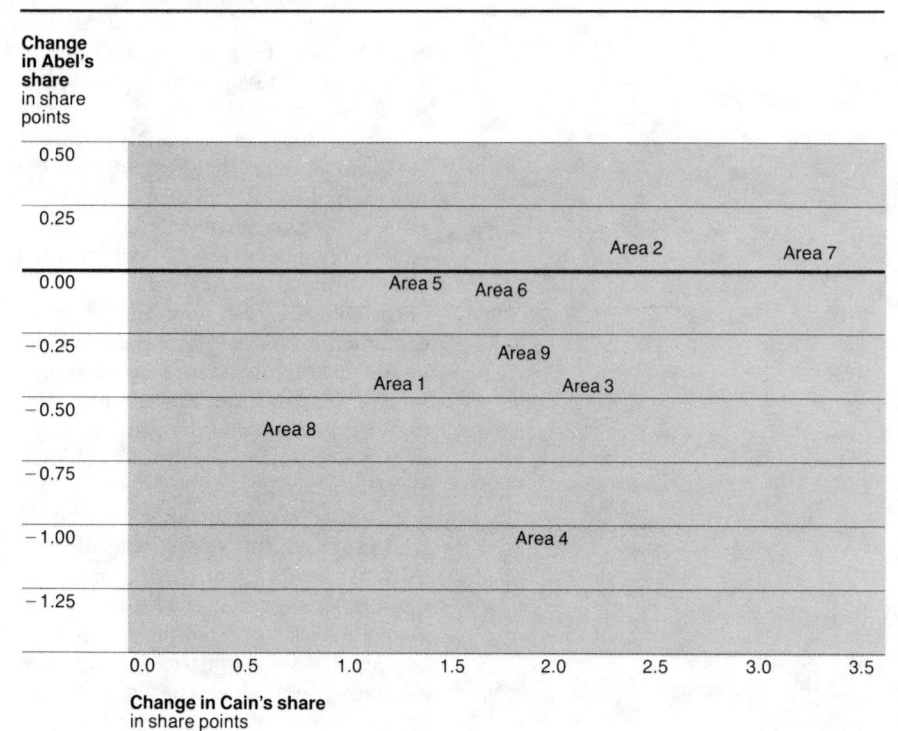

Exhibit V	**Regional market share changes, Abel and Cain** First half of 1981 in comparison with last half of 1980

Change in Abel's share in share points

```
 0.50 ┤
 0.25 ┤
                                    Area 2           Area 7
 0.00 ┤                    Area 5
                                 Area 6
-0.25 ┤                              Area 9
                        Area 1            Area 3
-0.50 ┤         Area 8
-0.75 ┤
-1.00 ┤                              Area 4
-1.25 ┤
       └────┬────┬────┬────┬────┬────┬────┬────┬
          0.0  0.5  1.0  1.5  2.0  2.5  3.0  3.5
```

Change in Cain's share in share points

---

was over. The advertising agency simply totaled the sales during the experiment and showed them in comparison with sales before the experiment for each of the treatments. It then concluded that magazines were the best media alternative.

One marketing scientist realized, however, that many factors aside from the media treatment could cause the results that the agency had found. He figured that something about the size of the cities might increase the sales of the product since the magazines happened to be in the largest cities. He then did a statistical analysis with multivariate procedures to isolate the effects of the population as well as the situations in which the experiment had been followed carelessly. He wanted to factor out the statistical effects of jointly having television and radio or television and magazines in some markets for some months.

With statistical precision, he discovered that television advertising is much more profitable than magazine advertising. In fact, using magazines may be no more profitable than using no advertising at all. As a result of this experiment, the company changed its media plan from using magazines heavily to using TV heavily. The company's advertising budget for the new product was $5 million.

How valuable was this experiment? It showed that the company could increase the productivity of its advertising by a factor of two or three. How much was this experiment worth? A lot more than it cost. Even if it had cost $500,000 or $1 million, it would have been worthwhile. Yet how many companies will ever consider spending $500,000 for a media experiment?

Analyzing cause and effect.
Knowing why your sales have changed in the past can be a very important aid in developing strategy for the future. Market response analysis is a complicated but effective way of analyzing past data. Nevertheless, a company needs a marketing scientist to ensure that conclusions will not be accepted without careful checking and analysis.

For example, when an over-the-counter drug company suffered a decline in its national unit market share for its drug "Abel," company officials attributed the falloff to the competitive efforts of two products. One, product "Baker," was a private-label product sold at half of Abel's price. The second, product "Cain," was produced by another division of Abel's company. The decision support system provided plots of national unit market share over time for all three products (see the three graphs in *Exhibit III*).

These graphs make clear that products Baker and Cain were taking share from product Abel. Statistical analysis of the numbers on the graphs confirmed that Abel's market share declines correlated with the share increases of Baker and Cain.

A marketing scientist demonstrated to the company's management, however, that this analysis and conclusions were faulty. If indeed Baker or Cain were competitive with Abel, then the competitive effects should be evident at the regional as well as the national level. As a test, the scientist developed several plots to relate the market share changes of product Abel with those of product Baker (see *Exhibit IV*) and of product Cain (see *Exhibit V*) by region for a six-month period. Each point in these exhibits represents market share changes for a specific region for two products. These scatter diagrams were also easy to obtain from the decision support system.

As shown in *Exhibit IV*, except for two observations associated with external events, the share decreases for Abel for a region were associated with the share increases for Baker for the same region. The evidence supported the national competitive effect at the regional level.

A similar plot for Cain, in *Exhibit V*, shows a very different story. In each region there was a tendency for Abel's share to decrease least where product Cain's share had increased the most. Conversely, the drug's share declined most in regions where Cain was also having its smallest share gains. Another unrelated, noncompetitive phenomenon was causing Abel's share decline. Cain could not have been caus-

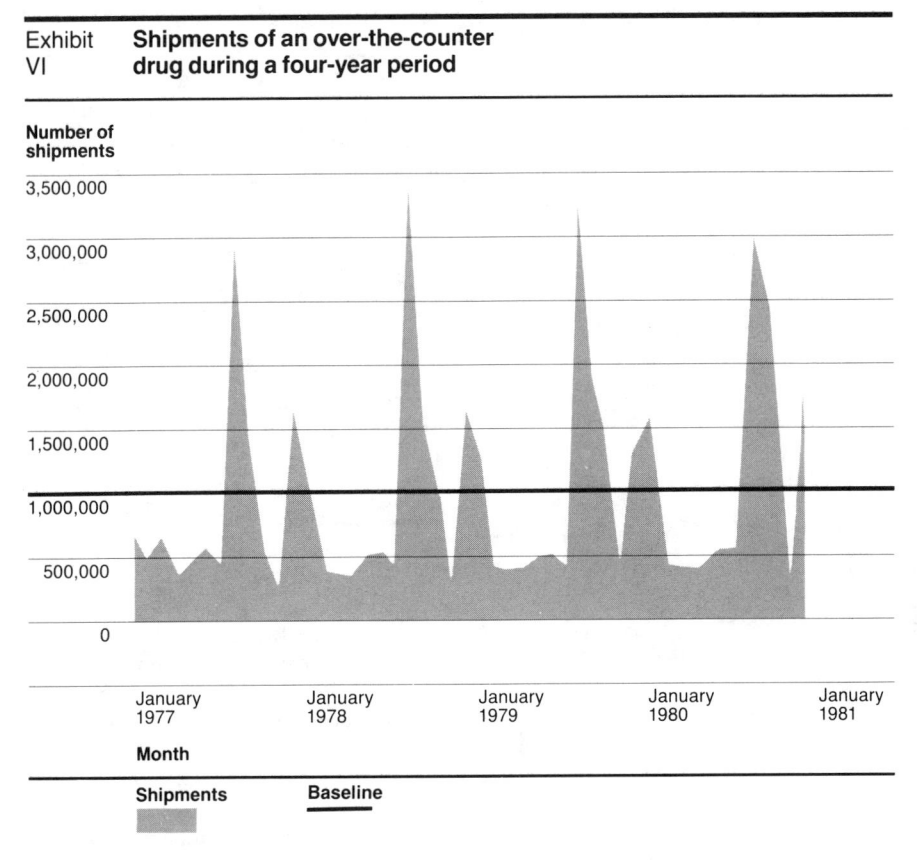

Exhibit VI	Shipments of an over-the-counter drug during a four-year period

Number of shipments

- 3,500,000
- 3,000,000
- 2,500,000
- 2,000,000
- 1,500,000
- 1,000,000
- 500,000
- 0

Month: January 1977, January 1978, January 1979, January 1980, January 1981

Shipments / Baseline

---

ing it; Cain was probably helping Abel by combining the two brands' sales force efforts. The marketing scientist's perceptive analysis stopped a potentially damaging interdivisional dispute and reoriented management's strategic thinking about competition.

In some cases the new technology may cause misinterpretation of marketing effectiveness because the data are not integrated with other pertinent information. For example, *Exhibit VI* is a graph that shows a marketing decision support system software program of monthly factory shipments for an over-the-counter drug. The spikes in the shipment data are associated with trade promotions, or temporary price reductions to the trade for a limited time. One module of the program produced the dotted line, which is an extrapolation of normal months to establish a baseline of what sales might have been had there been no promotion. Obviously, the trade promotions were very effective in stimulating sales.

Data from the same period but examined from another perspective suggest a very different conclusion.

Exhibit VII shows retailers' warehouse withdrawals for the same product and a similarly constructed baseline. Warehouse withdrawal data are much closer to consumer sales. This graph shows minimal effects from the trade promotions on sales to consumers. Indeed, the trade intermediaries in this case were simply using the promotional discount to stock up their warehouses with goods that they would have bought later at regular prices.

Until the warehouse withdrawal data were brought into the analysis, management was confident that the trade promotion program was highly profitable. After the new data were brought in, the managers changed their minds. This example illustrates the need to put all pertinent information in the same decision support system. Leaving even one data source out of consideration can be dangerous.

Minimizing the dangers.
What can management do to simultaneously reduce these dangers and take advantage of the potential that the new technology offers? At present, the computer terminal and television screen are not the best interface between management, which can be somewhat naive, and the new technology. Just because the technology makes using the computer terminal easy does not mean that the results will be perfectly correct or easy to implement. Persons with expertise in marketing science, employed either as full-time staff or as external consultants, can improve decision making when they serve as the liaison between the manager and the new technology.

The liaison people have two very important skills. They understand the business and the strategic problems that management faces. They also understand enough about data analysis, statistical analysis, and modeling to make sure that the appropriate checks and questions have been asked when a recommendation based on computer analysis is made. These people should report directly to top and middle management as part of staff groups. That way, they will control the quality of the analysis being done. We cannot emphasize enough the importance of having someone who understands data analysis review management's decisions on strategy.

Eventually this group of liaison people may be unnecessary. Ongoing artificial intelligence research will enable the computer to do as careful a market response analysis as a very good analyst. Until that happens, the liaison is important.

Taking advantage of the new data

To make optimal use of the new information, methods, and technologies, a company must combine the data, models, and tools of analysis. A marketing decision support system can do so. Its software and computers will help the organization translate data into information that is relevant to evaluating marketing decision alternatives.

The marketing decision support system software must be able to leverage all the latest data, models, and statistical analysis procedures. The software must have the capacity for data-base management, analysis, display, and modeling—all in a user-friendly environment. The data base should or-

| Exhibit VII | Warehouse withdrawals of an over-the-counter drug during a four-year period |

ganize information in ways that can be easily altered when situations or services change. For example, without doing massive reprogramming, a company must be able to incorporate new products or changes in sales districts into the data base. The software should have the capacity to allow many users to access the same integrated data base. The system needs a wide variety of output capabilities, ranging from simple tables to presentation-quality graphics and reports. To be able to divide and aggregate the data simultaneously into such categories as product, region, salesperson, and time period is very important.

Not only are simple "cuts" at the data necessary but also a wide variety of statistical and modeling capabilities to test and refine hypotheses generated by initial plots and tables of the data. We have seen many marketing decision support systems stop dead because the initial software selection did not anticipate how integrated, powerful, and flexible the software needs would be.[2]

To keep the system as productive as possible, it must have the support of an internal organization of specialized professionals as well as the sanction of top management. The support organization would carry out the following functions:

1 Install, operate, and maintain the computer hardware.
2 Administer the data base by recording which data are and which are not included in the system, updating the data base as new data became available, maintaining the documentation of available data, and ensuring data integrity.
3 Train administrators and users of the system at all levels of expertise and in all kinds of documentation needed.[3]

A typical company with a mature support organization might include six people besides the manager—two persons in computer operations, two in data-base administration, one to develop additional capabilities and support users, and one to train new employees.

Looking ahead

The future practice of marketing will bear little resemblance to that of the past. Changes in the managerial environment—the data, computers, human resources, and software—dictate a change in managerial practice.

Whereas a good marketing sense has led to many successful marketing careers, the future confronts us with the infusion of new marketing technologies and information sources. Appropriately supported, this new information will lead to a more accurate understanding of the business environment and to more profitable marketing strategies.

New, more powerful racing cars enable expert drivers to get around the Indianapolis Speedway increasingly faster. If these same cars are driven improperly, however, they will get into increasingly severe accidents. The same principle applies to the new data and computer technology. We must "drive" them with caution and the appropriate expertise.

Reprint 86112

---

2 For a detailed checklist of capabilities required in marketing decision support system software, see John D.C. Little and Michael N. Cassetari, "Appendix," *Decision Support for Marketing Managers* (New York: American Management Associations, 1984).

3 For more details, see Little and Cassetari, *Decision Support for Marketing Managers*.

'Backward' market research

Alan R. Andreasen

Mr. Andreasen is a visiting professor at the Graduate School of Management, University of California at Los Angeles, on leave from his position as professor of marketing at the University of Illinois at Champaign-Urbana. For HBR he has previously written on consumerism, on marketing in nonprofit organizations, and on low-cost market research.

An executive of an entertainment company decided that she knew too little about the consumer segments she was serving or hoped to serve. She had been practicing an obvious segmentation strategy aiming some programs at younger audiences, some at older ones, some at families, and some at singles. She needed a more sophisticated strategy, so she commissioned a research agency to analyze the company's market.

Despite high hopes, glowing promises, and the production of a glossy report heavy with statistics, the executive was disappointed in the findings. She said: "The research mostly told me things I already knew."

Her service operated in an industry whose primary consumers had already been studied more than 200 times. Each study said virtually the same thing as this one: the audience was largely female, economically upscale, well educated, urban, and mainly on either end of the age distribution scale.

"Even where the results were new," she said, "they didn't tell me what I needed to know so I could use them." The consumer profile relied on demographics as the principal segmentation variable. "Sure," the manager added, "I know that men attend less than women, but why? Do they see fewer benefits than women or are there barriers to attendance that apply to men and not to women? And what about the age differences? Does the middle-aged group drop out because we don't meet their needs or are they just into things that we can't match, like building a family?" She had learned who her customers were *not* but nothing about how to motivate them.

"When the researcher tried to explain the results, it was obvious he hadn't understood what I wanted. The results were all a bit off the mark." An example was the measurement of loyalty. The researcher assumed his client wanted a behavioral measure, so he sought information on the proportion of recent purchases that were from each competitor and on recent brand-switching patterns. But she also wanted an attitudinal measure revealing consumer intentions. She wanted to know less about their past loyalty than about their likely future loyalty.

How it goes wrong

We can sympathize with this executive's complaints, although clearly she must share the blame for poor study design. She neglected to make the undertaking a real collaboration with the researcher. This is a common fault. Indeed, studies of research successes and failures point again and again to close collaboration between researcher and client as the single most important factor predicting a good outcome.

The typical approach of the two parties starts with defining the problem. Then they translate the problem into a research methodology. This leads to the development of research instruments, a sampling plan, coding and interviewing instructions, and other details. The researcher takes to the field, examines the resulting data, and writes a report.

The executive then steps in to translate the researcher's submissions into action. She has of course already devoted some thought to application of the results. From my observation, however, before the research is undertaken the intended action is left vague and general. Managers tend to define the research problem as a broad area of ignorance. They say in effect: "Here are some things I don't know. When the results come in, I'll know more. And when I know more, then I can figure out what to do." In my experience, this approach makes it highly likely that the findings will be off target.

What I suggest is a procedure that turns the traditional approach to research design on its head. This procedure, a proven one, stresses close collaboration between researcher and corporate decision makers. It markedly raises the odds that the company will come up with findings that are not only "interesting" but also lead to actionable conclusions.

There are only two cases in which research is not expected to be immediately actionable. The first is when the research is intended to be basic – that is, to lay the groundwork for later investigation or action rather than have any near-term impact. The second occasion is when the research is methodological – that is, it is designed to improve the organization's ability to ask questions in the future. Except for these two instances, research should be designed to lead to a decision.

Turned on its head

The "backward" approach I advocate rests on the premise that the best way to design usable research is to start where the process usually ends and then work backward. So we develop each stage of the design on the basis of what comes after it, not before. The procedure is as follows:

1   Determine how the research results will be implemented (which helps to define the problem).

2   To ensure the implementation of the results, determine what the

© 1985 by the President and Fellows of Harvard College, all rights reserved.

final report should contain and how it should look.

3 Specify the analyses necessary to "fill in the blanks" in the research report.

4 Determine the kind of data that must be assembled to carry out these analyses.

5 Scan the available secondary sources and/or syndicated services to see whether the specified data already exist or can be obtained quickly and cheaply from others. (While you are at it, observe how others have tried to meet data needs like your own.)

6 If no such easy way out presents itself, design instruments and a sampling plan that will yield the data to fit the analyses you have to undertake.

7 Carry out the field work, continually checking to see whether the data will meet your needs.

8 Do the analysis, write the report, and watch it have its intended effect.

As one might expect, the first step is the most important.

Step 1. As I mentioned before, to most managers the research "problem" is seen as a lack of important facts about their marketing environment. A manager may say, "The problem is I don't know if formula A is preferred over formula B." Or, "The problem is I don't know if my distributors are more satisfied with my organization than my competitor's distributors are with theirs, and if they aren't, what they're unhappy about."

In this way of defining the problem, the "solution" is simply a reduction in the level of ignorance. The data elicited may be very "interesting" and may give managers a great deal of satisfaction in revealing things they didn't know. But satisfaction can quickly turn to frustration and disappointment when the executive tries to use the results.

Take for example a life-style study done not long ago on over-the-counter drugs. Some respondents, who claimed they were always getting colds and the flu, were very pessimistic about their health. They frequently went to doctors but the doctors were never much help. They thought that OTC drugs were often very beneficial but they weren't sure why. This information, together with other details, caused the researchers to label this group "the hypochondriacs."

What to do with these results? As is usually the case with segmentation strategies, there are quantity and quality decisions to make. The company has to decide whether to pump more marketing resources into the hypochondriac group than its proportion of the population would justify. The marketing VP might first say yes because the hypochondriacs are heavy drug users.

But the picture is more complicated than that. Perhaps hypochondriacs are sophisticated buyers, set in their purchase patterns, and very loyal to favorite brands. If so, money aimed at them would have little impact on market share. Light users, on the other hand, may have fragile loyalties and throwing money at them could entice them to switch brands. Of course, just the opposite might be true: the hypochondriacs, being heavy users, might prove very impressionable and responsive to compelling ads.

On the qualitative side, life-style research could be much more helpful. Since it generates a rich profile describing each group's jobs, families, values, and preferences, this research could tell the company what to say. But the frustrated manager is likely not to know where to say these things. There is no *Hypochondriac's Journal* in which to advertise, and there may be no viewing and reading patterns that don't apply to heavy users in general—hypochondriacs or not.

A self-selection strategy could be tried wherein the company develops an ad speaking to hypochondriacs' fears and worries in the hope that they will see the message and say to themselves, "Ah, they're talking about me!" But nonhypochondriac heavy users who read the ad might say, "Well, if this product is really for those wimpy worrywarts, it certainly is not for sensible, rational me! I'll take my patronage elsewhere." In this case the research will be very interesting (fine fodder for cocktail party banter) but not actionable.

But suppose that the company had first laid out all the action alternatives it might take after the study. If the marketing VP had made it clear that his problems were (a) whether to allocate marketing dollars differently and (b) whether to develop marketing campaigns aimed at particular, newly discovered segments, he would have set the project in a more appropriate direction.

In the first case, discussions with the researcher would help the VP determine the criteria that would justify a different allocation. Naturally, before he can reach a decision the VP needs research on the likely responses of different segments to advertising and promotional money spent on them. In the second case, the manager needs to know whether there are indeed channels for best reaching these segments. Only by first thinking through the decisions to be made with the research results will the project be started with high likelihood of actionability.

Step 2. After Step 1, management should ask itself: What should the final report look like so that we'll know exactly what moves to make when the report is in? Now the collaboration between the researcher and the manager should intensify and prove dynamic and exceedingly creative.

Scenarios are a good technique for developing ideas for the contents of the report. The initiative here lies with the researcher, who generates elements of a hypothetical report and then confronts management with tough questions like: "If I came up with this cross-tabulation with these numbers in it, what would you do?"

The first payoff from this exercise arises from improvement of the research itself. These results can take us forward by sharpening the decision alternatives and backward by indicating the best design for the questionnaire or how the analysis of the findings should be carried out. The forward effect is evident in this case:

A product manager, marketing a high-priced convenience good, is considering cancellation of a multiple-purchase discount because she thinks that most people taking advantage of it are loyal customers who are already heavy users, are upscale, and are largely price inelastic. Therefore, she speculates, the discount mainly represents lost revenue. To decide this question, one must of course predict the responses of old and new customers to the elimination of the discounts. The researcher hypothesizes tables showing various results.

Suppose the first iteration shows long-time customers to be price inelastic and new customers to be price elastic. This result suggests to the product manager the advisability of forgoing no discounts except a one-time offer to consumers who have never tried the product. In considering this alternative, the manager will realize that before she can reach a decision she needs to know whether potential new customers can be reached with the special offer in a way that will minimize (or, better, foreclose) purchases at a discount by long-time customers.

This new formulation of the decision leads to a discussion of results set out in another set of dummy tables showing responsiveness to the one-time discount by past patron behavior. Other tables would then reveal what television shows various consumer segments watch and what they read or listen to, which will indicate whether they are differentially reachable. And so goes the process of recycling between the decision context and the research design.

The recycling will reveal what research is needed. Sometimes the researcher will present contrasting tables or regression results pointing in a certain direction, only to discover that management is most likely to take the same course of action no matter what the results. This is usually a prima facie case for doing away with that part of the research design altogether.

Participation in the design decisions has other advantages. It serves to co-opt managers into supporting the work and deepen their understanding of many of the details of the research. That understanding permits the researcher to simplify the report immeasurably. Working with contrasting, hypothetical tables can make the manager eager for the findings and unlikely to be startled by surprising results. Participation will also help reveal to management any limitations of the study. In my experience, managers are often tempted to go far beyond research "truth" when implementing the results, especially if the reported truth supports the course of action they prefer to take anyway.

Step 3. The form of the report will clearly dictate the nature of the analysis. If management is leery of multivariate analysis, the researchers should design a series of step-by-step cross-tabulations. If management is comfortable with the higher reaches of statistics, the researcher can draw out some of the more advanced analytic procedures. In general, however, the analysis phase should be straightforward. If the exercise of scenario writing has gone well, the analysis should amount to little more than filling in the blanks.

Step 4. The backward approach is very helpful in data gathering. One large electronics manufacturer wanted to gauge young consumers' knowledge of and preferences for stereo components. Not until the researcher had prepared mock tables, showing preference data by age and sex, did the client's wishes become clear. By "young" the client meant children as young as ten. Moreover, the client believed that preteens, being a very volatile group, undergo radical changes from year to year, especially as they approach puberty.

Design plans to set a low-age cutoff for the sample at 13 and to group respondents by age category—such as 13 to 16 and 17 to 20—went out the window. If the researcher had been following the usual design approach, the client's expectations may not have surfaced until the study was well under way.

Backward design can also help determine the appropriateness of using strict probability sampling techniques. If, for example, management wants to project certain findings into some universe, the research must employ precise probability methods. On the other hand, if the client is chiefly interested in frequency counts (say, of words used by consumers to describe the company's major brands or of complaints voiced about its salespeople), sampling restrictions need not be so tight. In my experience, researchers often build either too much or too little sampling quality for the uses the company has in mind. Similarly, scenario writing will usually also reveal that management wants more breakdowns of the results, requiring larger sample sizes or more precise stratification procedures than initially planned. Through simulating the application of the findings, the final research design is much more likely to meet management's needs and permit low field costs.

Steps 5-8. The first four steps encompass the major advantages of the backward technique. Steps 5 through 8 revert to a traditional forward approach that applies the research decisions and judgments made earlier. If all parties have collaborated well in the early stages, the last four steps will carry through what has already been largely determined.

More informed decisions

What I propose here is a technique that requires marketing executives to give up their valuable time so that market research can be made more valuable. Great benefits can accrue thereby:

The organization can avoid research that will not benefit decision making.

Research results that *are* produced will be actionable.

Surprising conclusions can be anticipated and contingency plans developed.

Sample designs will be only as sophisticated as the organization's data needs warrant, and therefore more efficient.

Sample sizes will be large enough (or stratified appropriately) to allow more precise analyses of the main subgroups of interest.

Questions will be worded as management *really* wants them.

Management, being closely involved in the research design, is more likely to support the implementation phases and take quick action on the research results when they finally become available.

This procedure takes time for both managers and researchers. But determining where you want to go, then working backward to figure out how to get there, is likely to yield more valuable data leading to fruitful decisions.

Reprint 85301

Growing Concerns

Topics of particular interest to owners and managers of smaller businesses

Edited by David E. Gumpert

Cost-conscious marketing research

Alan R. Andreasen

Among managers of small businesses and nonprofit organizations, the term marketing research *frequently conjures up images of lengthy surveys, complicated mathematics, and, above all, high price tags. To many, marketing research is something understandable and affordable only to managers of large companies. The author contends that such images spring from five misconceptions. He advises managers to consider alternatives to the full-length, expensive survey as legitimate forms of marketing research—techniques such as test marketing, focus group interviews, visual observations, and the use of secondary sources. More important than the research approach, he contends, is the relationship of the information desired to the decision to be reached. Managers can often get what they want from research without using sophisticated means or going to great expense.*

Mr. Andreasen is professor of marketing at the University of Illinois in Champaign-Urbana. His most recent HBR article was published last year—"Nonprofits: Check Your Attention to Customers" (May-June). Prior to that he wrote, with Arthur Best, "Consumers Complain—Does Business Respond?" for HBR's July-August 1977 issue.

Many small businesses and nonprofit organizations assiduously avoid more than a cursory flirtation with marketing research because they misunderstand what it is and what it can accomplish. Five misconceptions often dominate managers' thinking about it:

1 The "big decision" myth. You turn to marketing research only when you have a major decision to make; otherwise it has little to do with the details of day-to-day decision making.

2 The "survey myopia" myth. With its random samples, questionnaires, computer printouts, and statistical analyses, marketing research is synonymous with field survey research.

3 The "big bucks" myth. Marketing research is so expensive that it can only be used by the wealthiest organizations, and then only for their major decisions.

4 The "sophisticated researcher" myth. Since research involves complex and advanced technology, only trained experts can and should pursue it.

5 The "most research is not read" myth. A very high proportion of marketing research is irrelevant to managers or simply confirms what they already know. Often the research is so poorly designed and written up or so esoteric that it simply ends up in the bottom drawer.

In this article I consider each of the myths and show why they are misleading. Then I suggest several approaches to low-cost research.

The 'big decision' myth

Too often, marketing research is deemed necessary only for decisions involving large financial stakes and in such cases should always be carried out. But research should be viewed from a cost-benefit perspective. Its costs are usually of two types—the expenses for the research itself and the amount of lost sales and lost competitive advantage caused by delaying a decision until the results are in. The benefits result from improving the quality of decisions under consideration. Any improvement, in turn, is a function of the stakes involved and how uncertain you are about the rightness of your course of action. Note that the benefits of research are proportional to the manager's uncertainty about which way to go, not to the uncertainty about the future.

The cost-benefit ratio may often come out against research even when the stakes are high. Take the case of the restaurant manager thinking of adding a line of Mexican dishes to the menu and investing in a series of advertisements to promote this innovation. He called in a research professional to design a study of local food preferences that would show how likely acceptance of the repositioning strategy would be. Although such a study could cost several thousand dollars, the researcher determined in extended discussions with the manager that unless the survey found virtually no interest in Mexican food in the area, the manager was going ahead with the decision to add the line.

The manager was highly uncertain about the market, but he *was* certain that this decision was best.

The researcher convinced the manager that the research expenditure was unnecessary and that the money could more productively be used to ensure that the new line got the advertising send-off it needed to have the best chances of succeeding.

On the other hand, research can be justified even when the amount at stake is not very great. This is the case whenever the research can be done inexpensively, will not take very long to complete, and will help clarify which actions to take.

These conditions often accompany advertising copy decisions. While total expenditures are small, managers do usually have two or three candidate ads, each of which seems to have potential worth. Showing the ads to a small but representative set of prospective target customers – very modest research – usually reveals one superior candidate or at least, by pointing out serious defects in one or two candidate ads, allows a narrowing of the choice. This process has a fringe benefit in that once in a while it produces extremely good suggestions for entirely different ads.

Research may also be justifiable when the stakes initially appear modest but later turn out to have been undervalued. In this regard, it is generally useful to think through the monetary consequences of making a poor decision. When one considers the possible side effects of a bad decision on such things as the organization's reputation, its ability to attract funding and staff, and its sales of related products, the costs may be very high indeed. Such is often the case when small businesses or nonprofits venture beyond their national borders and assume that what works in their home countries will work overseas. The international community is replete with horror stories of marketing gaffes with long-term consequences that could have been avoided with a little research.

You may grant the argument thus far but then assert that there is no low-cost research to meet these challenges, that the suggestions for research made previously involve the proverbial quick-and-dirty study that may well be worse than no research at all. The only good research, you say, is a survey carefully done. This contention leads me to the second major misconception about the use of research.

The 'survey myopia' myth

Any reliable information that improves marketing decisions can be considered marketing research. If you take this view, many alternatives to formal survey research come to mind. Consider the entrepreneur thinking of introducing a new service but having no idea whether the target market will accept the service or, even with acceptance, how quickly it can be expected to reach break-even. If successful, the new service would yield a contribution to profits of only a few thousand dollars in the first few years. The entrepreneur could conduct a survey to reduce this uncertainty. However, to make the research 95% certain of being within two percentage points of the break-even market share figure of 10%, the entrepreneur must make the sample size 900.

An experienced survey researcher would estimate that, assuming the questionnaire and sampling plan are already designed and ignoring analysis and report preparation costs, simply completing the interviews would cost between $3,000 and $7,000. (The amount would depend on the duration and type of interviews done.)

Clearly, such research would eat up the entrepreneur's initial years' contribution profits. More important is the question whether the research would yield valid data in any case. That is, one should ask whether it is reasonable to expect respondents to be candid about or even to know their likely behavior with respect to this new service, especially if many feel it would not be gracious to disappoint the interviewer or the research sponsor by showing little enthusiasm for the venture.

How else, then, might the survey research objectives be achieved at lower cost? The company can try test marketing in representative markets. This approach has the virtue of not only lowering costs but yielding useful data (that is, it shows what people *will* do, not what they *say* they will do). Testing in a number of markets also allows alternative marketing strategies to be systematically evaluated.

Another low-cost approach is the commissioning of focus group interviews of 8 to 12 members of the target audience at a time. Although the results are not strictly projectable to the larger market because the groups are not randomly selected, these results do cut the cost of interviewing by a quarter or a half. Interviewers can sometimes develop richer data in the relaxed, chatty format of the focus group.

Also, the groups can at least alert management to problems with the new service that would sabotage its introduction, as they might in foreign markets. When a company uses several focus group sessions covering the range of people likely to be target market members for the new venture, officials can spot serious problems mentioned by a modest number of participants and abort a service or product launching. Elaborate probability sampling designs are simply not necessary to satisfy this objective.

The 'big bucks' myth

Marketing research is much more diverse than the inexperienced observer would think. There are many inexpensive alternatives to surveys:

1 **Systematic observation.** Managers can obtain many kinds of marketing data simply by carefully observing behavior. Retailers have found pedestrian and vehicle traffic counts to be invaluable in assessing the success of competitors' new products or services and in evaluating new outlet locations. To gauge the effectiveness of in-store displays or packages, a staff person can record patrons' reactions. The video cameras now commonly installed for security can also be used for this purpose.

Managers can determine the relative importance of outlet or product features by recording customers' questions and comments in the outlets themselves. Automobile dealers and service station managers have studied their customers' radio station preferences simply by observing the dial settings of cars brought in for service. Salespeople who regularly visit customers can record their reactions to new offers and their future purchase plans as well as take advantage of their knowlege about competitors' plans.

Note that what distinguishes marketing research from casual observation or a "feel" for the market is careful specification of the needed observations, systematic observation, observation at random times and places (where possible, by a variety of observers), and careful recording and analysis of results.

2 **Secondary sources.** Industry, government, and academic reports and papers often yield data on similar ventures tried elsewhere. Reports of case studies may alert managers to fatal defects.

A medium-sized art museum, for example, learned the value of researching the experience of others when it was planning a program to expose low-income children to the art world. To launch this program, the museum director tried to kill two birds with one stone by inviting government supporters, private sponsors, and influential citizens to observe the first night's "encounter with culture" and see firsthand what a noble enterprise they were associated with. Before proceeding, however, the director conducted an informal telephone survey of museums in other cities to determine if they had staged similar events. What she learned caused her to change her plans drastically.

Another museum that tried the very same approach reported disastrous results. It found that its supporters were horrified to observe children of low-income families hollering and tearing about in the hallowed museum corridors—quite natural behavior for children—and actually touching the statues and other works of art. Mr. and Mrs. Uppercrust, who had given $500,000 for the Jean Tinguely kinetic sculpture, were not at all pleased to see enthusiastic ghetto youths giving the Tinguely kinetics a little help. Donations dropped sharply (although no one ever said anything), and many months and careful countermarketing were needed to overcome the harm.

Secondary data may also provide information about the time needed to gain acceptance. In most cases, entrepreneurs searching through secondary sources can often make effective use of library-based computerized information retrieval systems.

3 **Archival research.** Valuable marketing research data are already available to many organizations and are simply waiting to be analyzed by the enterprising entrepreneur. For example, owners can glean very good insights into competitors' advertising strategies or pricing practices from a trip to the local newspaper and from scanning past issues of the paper selected at random. Zip code data on existing charge customers can yield much about the geographic dispersion and travel patterns of a store's or a theater's customers and, when supplemented by census data, can indicate income, education, and other household characteristics of these customers.

4 **Systematic experimentation.** Many regular marketing efforts of small businesses and nonprofit organizations are amenable to experimental manipulation. For example, by varying themes in routine fund-raising mailings, a nonprofit manager can accumulate a great deal of scientifically validated information about which marketing strategies work and which do not. Also, newspaper advertisements can be varied so that the managers will learn the effects of ad size, the ratio of white space to copy, and the use of photographs.

Even if a survey must be done, managers can reduce research costs with these approaches:

☐ Convenience samples involving systematic querying of customer contacts, for example. Such samples are often adequate for many exploratory research purposes to identify potential marketing problems or to develop advertising or new product ideas. Indeed, many organizations miss important opportunities for collecting data from those with whom they regularly come in contact. Salespeople can easily query customers coming to an outlet, hospital officials can interview patients, and anyone can ask opinion leaders met at meetings or cocktail parties questions about current managerial concerns.

The success of such surveys depends on careful formulation of the questions in advance, recognition of biases, thoroughness in carrying out the questioning, and systematic recording and analysis of the results.

☐ Snowball sampling, which is the expansion of a convenience sample of present customers by a manager who asks respondents to suggest others to query. Although obviously a biased procedure, snowball sampling has several advantages. If you use the original respondents' names in an introduction to the second set of interviewees, you can significantly improve the chances of getting their cooperation in your research.

Furthermore, the demographics and life-style characteristics of the second sample are likely to resemble those of the original respondents. The new sample will differ in one respect only: the respondents will not be regular customers or contacts of the surveying organization.

Snowball sampling is also a unique way to find rare populations. Customers for particular low-volume products and services can often point the way to others who could be surveyed—others who already have these items and services or are thinking of obtaining them from competitors.

☐ Omnibus surveys, which commercial research suppliers conduct regularly. They can often include a few key questions of interest to a marketing manager. The costs per question can be kept low since several clients share them. And, if you are from a legitimate nonprofit organization, some research suppliers may, at little or no cost, include a few questions on an omnibus survey as a public service.

Sometimes volunteers and colleges are willing to help carry out such research. Many nonprofit organizations regularly have access to pools of volunteers—through local service clubs, for instance. You can assign a few such volunteers to routine survey responsibilities, see that they are trained in survey techniques, and closely supervise their work. The volunteers should be treated as professionals, not as unpaid helpers. As noted earlier, bad research is often much worse than no research at all.

Many colleges that have marketing research courses are seeking businesses to serve as field survey research cases for term projects. Again, the key is to make certain that these inexperienced researchers are carefully trained and supervised.

The 'sophisticated researcher' myth

Just as marketing research need not involve complex sampling and elaborate designs, and indeed often purposely lacks randomization, so a high level of sophistication in sampling techniques, statistics, and computer analysis is not essential. Of course, executives of small businesses and nonprofits planning to undertake programs of research should acquaint themselves with at least the rudimentary principles of random sampling, questionnaire design, and graphic presentation of results.

Even when managers need high levels of sophistication—for example, if elaborate experiments or careful field study projects are being planned—they can get low-cost assistance on an ad hoc basis. Professors at local colleges are one resource. An alternative particularly appropriate to nonprofit organizations is the voluntary help of local professional researchers. Smaller companies and nonprofits contemplating extended research programs may want to ask marketing research professionals to sit on their boards of directors.

The 'most research is not read' myth

Unfortunately, executives who would rather not bother with research or who subconsciously fear the results use this rationale for their inaction. Poor research certainly does occur, but when it does it is usually a testimonial to poor planning. In my experience, no piece of well-planned research has ever been rejected as unhelpful, although it may be ignored on other, often political, grounds.

How can one ensure that research will not be wasted effort? The answer rests with both the manager requesting the research and the researcher doing it. Research will be most valuable when:

1   It is undertaken after the manager has made clear to the researcher what the decision alternatives are and what it is about those decisions that necessitates additional information.

2   The relationship between the results and the decision is clearly understood. For the manager, the researcher should prepare hypothetical tables of results indicating likely outcomes for the proposed effort. Depending on the manager's reactions to the tables, revisions can be made to bring the research on target.

3   The results are communicated well. If hypothetical results are presented, the manager should become quite familiar with the intricacies of the research design and be able to appreciate the nuances of the findings when they are finally produced.

Research need not be intimidating. It can play an important role in effective management. While research is not appropriate to all business decisions, it shouldn't be neglected just because managers of small businesses and nonprofits entertain myths about the process. Rather, executives should be prepared to carefully analyze the particular conditions under which research of various kinds is warranted and to consider the wide range of possible low-cost designs. The payoffs from a less myopic approach to the marketing research function can be substantial. ▽

Reprint 83401

Special Report

Market research the Japanese way

Johny K. Johansson and Ikujiro Nonaka

When Sony researched the market for a lightweight portable cassette player, results showed that consumers wouldn't buy a tape recorder that didn't record. Company chairman Akio Morita decided to introduce the Walkman anyway, and the rest is history. Today it's one of Sony's most successful products.

Japanese companies *do* use surveys — but they trust their instincts first.

Morita's disdain for large-scale consumer surveys and other scientific research tools isn't unique in Japan. Matsushita, Toyota, and other well-known Japanese consumer goods companies are just as skeptical about the Western style of market research. Occasionally, the Japanese do conduct consumer attitude surveys, but most executives don't base their marketing decisions on them or on other popular techniques. As the head of Matsushita's videocassette recorder division once said, "Why do Americans do so much marketing research? You can find out what you need by traveling around and visiting the retailers who carry your product."

Hands-on research

Of course, Japanese corporations want accurate and useful information about their markets as much as U.S. and European companies do. They just go about it differently. Japanese executives put much more faith in information they get directly from wholesalers and retailers in the distribution channels. Moreover, they track what's happening among channel members on a monthly, weekly, and sometimes even daily basis.

Japanese-style market research relies heavily on two kinds of information: "soft data" obtained from visits to dealers and other channel members, and "hard data" about shipments, inventory levels, and retail sales. Japanese managers believe that these data better reflect the behavior and intentions of flesh-and-blood consumers.

Japanese companies want information that is context specific rather than context free — that is, data directly relevant to consumer attitudes about the product, or to the way buyers have used or will use specific products, rather than research results that are too remote from actual consumer behavior to be useful. When Japanese companies do conduct surveys, they interview consumers who have actually bought or used a product. They do not scrutinize an undifferentiated mass public to learn about general attitudes and values. When Toyota wanted to learn what Americans preferred in small, imported cars, for example, the company asked owners and others who had driven the car what they liked or disliked about the Volkswagen Beetle.

Soft-data gathering. Senior as well as middle-level Japanese managers get involved in gathering soft data because they see the information as critical both for market entry and for maintaining good relationships later. Though impressionistic, such hands-on data give the managers a distinctive feel for the market — something they believe surveys or quantitative research methods can't supply. Talks with dealers yield realistic, context-specific information about competitors' as well as their own market performance.

A good example is Canon's decision on a new U.S. distribution strategy. In the early 1970s, the company's senior management became concerned about U.S. camera sales. Other product lines were doing well, but camera sales had lost ground to the chief competitor, Minolta. Canon finally decided it needed its own sales subsidiary because its distributor, Bell & Howell, wouldn't give additional support for the Canon line. Senior managers didn't

A professor at the University of Washington's Graduate School of Business Administration, Johny K. Johansson has done research in marketing strategy, advertising management, international marketing, and Japanese business. Ikujiro Nonaka is a professor at the Institute for Business Research at Hitotsubashi University in Tokyo. He has published six books on management and organization and with Hirotaka Takeuchi wrote "The New New Product Development Game" (HBR January-February 1986).

use a broad survey of consumers or retailers to make this decision. They sent three managers to the United States to look into the problem and changed strategies based on their observations.

To learn the market, track the channels.

Canon's head of the U.S. team himself spent almost six weeks in 1972 visiting camera stores and other retail outlets across the United States. From talks with store owners, Tatehiro Tsuruta learned that U.S. dealers weren't giving Canon much support because their sales forces were too small. He also found out what kinds of cameras and promotional support would get them excited about the company's line.

This soft-data approach appears to lack the methodological rigor of scientific market research, but it's by no means haphazard or careless. In fact, Tsuruta's results were more meaningful because he actually observed how consumers behaved in the stores and how salespeople responded. On entering a store, Tsuruta would act as if he were just a customer browsing around. He would note how the cameras were displayed and how the store clerks served customers. Then by simply asking "What cameras do you stock?" he could assess whether the dealer was enthusiastic or indifferent about the Canon line. He could also determine how knowledgeable people were about camera features.

Tsuruta would then identify himself and invite the store manager to lunch to discuss cameras and whatever else happened to be on the dealer's mind. The payoff was more than just market research. He was building lasting relationships with the dealers—an important competitive advantage.

When Tsuruta visited drugstores and other discount outlets that Minolta favored, he could see that these markets wouldn't work for Canon. Customers got poor service—in part because salespeople knew little about the products they were selling. The mass merchandisers' heavy price competition also made it difficult to project a quality image.

Tsuruta's research decided Canon's distribution strategy: sell exclusively through specialty dealers serving an upscale, high-quality niche just below Nikon's targeted segment. The successful introduction of Canon's AE-1 camera in 1976 proved the strategy right.

Canon is by no means unique among Japanese companies in the sales and distribution problems it experienced in the United States or in the means it used to remedy them. A group of managers Honda sent to the United States in 1965 learned to their surprise that few dealers there stocked and serviced motorcycles exclusively. Company executives realized they would have to develop their own dealer network. Sony entered the U.S. radio and TV market in the late 1950s and almost immediately decided to establish its own U.S. distributor so it could be sure to get adequate sales support.

This soft-data approach is popular even after a Japanese company has penetrated the market. Frequent visits to people on the distribution channel help manufacturers resolve problems before they escalate and damage sales or relationships. Isao Makino, president of Toyota's U.S. sales subsidiary from 1975 to 1983—a period of great gains in market share—used to visit every Toyota dealer in the United States at least once a year. "I found," he said, "that out of the ten complaints from each dealer, you could attribute about five or six to simple misunderstandings, another two or three could be solved on the spot, and only one or two needed further work."

Hard-data gathering. When Japanese managers want hard data to compare their products to competitors', they look at inventory, sales, and other information that show the items' actual movement through the channels. Then they visit channel members at both the retail and wholesale levels to analyze sales and distribution coverage reports, monthly product movement records (weekly for some key stores), plant-to-wholesaler shipment figures, and syndicated turnover and shipment statistics on competitors.

Japanese managers routinely monitor their markets at home and abroad this way. Consider how Matsushita dealt with the weak performance of its Panasonic line distributor in South Africa. The sales figures he reported were reasonable, but he couldn't produce reliable data on sales and shares for the various types of stores or on inventory levels in the distribution chain.

In early 1982, three managers from the company's household electronics division paid a call on the South African distributor. Then they dropped in on the distributor's retail stores and wholesale facilities. Customarily, after exchanging greetings and presenting a token gift from headquarters, they got right down to business. They asked to see inventory, shipment, and sales records as part of a complete store audit covering Matsushita and competitive products. Six weeks later, after analyzing all the data, they gave the incredulous distributor a complete picture of Panasonic's product movement and market share through the entire South African channel. They also told the distributor what figures he should collect and report to the home office in the future.

Monitoring the channels

Japanese managers try to track changing customer tastes closely and quickly. Their "one step at a time" management style for decision making also applies to how they approach marketing. After analyzing both hard and soft data on their channels, they make small, incremental changes in product features, packaging, and promotional efforts. Awareness of what's happening in the channels on a weekly or even daily basis gives them a deep and focused understanding of the marketplace and enables them to fine-tune their marketing rapidly – thereby protecting their competitive edge. This skill is especially important in the highly competitive packaged goods and consumer durable goods markets.

Kao Corporation, which dominates the detergent and soap market in Japan, illustrates this tight channel monitoring and incremental changes in marketing strategies. Kao executives analyze point-of-sales data weekly and wholesale inventory and sales statistics monthly.

The company occasionally uses consumer surveys and other quantitative research tools, but executives never base marketing decisions primarily on the information from them. These findings merely trigger more thorough audits of the channels using both soft- and hard-data gathering. If a survey or household panel study, for example, shows a sudden change in brand preferences or in family purchase patterns, Kao will send a high-level management team out to the stores. The group will spend one day at each store just observing customer behavior. The next day the team will talk to the store owner or manager to learn what kinds of support will move the products better. They'll also ask if the dealer needs help stocking shelves or if special promotions would help.

Such tight channel monitoring has paid off handsomely for Kao, among others. When Procter & Gamble introduced disposable diapers in Japan in the mid-1970s, it immediately took 90% of this new and growing market. Lured by the big sales and earnings potential, Uni Charm, Kao, and other Japanese manufacturers created their own lines. With tight channel monitoring, the Japanese could quickly change product features to better suit consumer tastes, and by 1984 P&G's market share had plummeted to an anemic 8%.

One factor that frustrates U.S. and other Western corporations' efforts to enter Japanese distribution channels is their lack of knowledge about distributor expectations, which limits their ability to respond to con-

---

You can't teach marketing in school – you learn it in the field.

---

sumer tastes. The handicapped Westerners can't refine their marketing quickly enough in Japan to parry competitors' moves.

Tight channel monitoring also improves operations and cost control. Kao and other Japanese companies would never be caught with the kind of inventory pileups that Warner Communications' Atari subsidiary found itself saddled with in 1983. A six-month lag in reports from retailers led to disastrous inventory levels of TV game cassettes.

Strong vertical integration. Japanese companies exert considerably more control over their distribution channels than do most U.S. and European corporations. Toyota has been more successful than Nissan in the Japanese market because of its stronger distribution network. In many cases, this control is nearly absolute because the manufacturer actually owns the distributors or has sufficient market power to dominate the channel. Shiseido, for example, a cosmetics manufacturer, has a strong market presence in Japan. It sells through a network of independent stores that use company-trained salespeople and reserve exclusive shelf space for the company's brands. In Japan, a consumer's choice of store often dictates what brand he or she will buy.

Such strong vertical integration affects the kind and quality of market research information Japanese managers can gather. They can shift some research tasks to the dealers, for example. It's not unusual for store employees to survey Japanese households by mail or phone, interview people when they come into a store, or even visit customers' homes for a talk.

Japanese salespeople change jobs less often than U.S. and European retail employees, so they are in a better position to develop expertise about customers and competitors. Moreover, stores tend to remain in the same locations. When Matsushita wants information on its Japanese customers, it goes to its 4,000 retail stores to find out.

Generalist managers. Few Japanese managers at all corporate levels have received a formal business education; it is still something of a novelty in Japan. Other than Keio Business School, only a few business institutes exist there, and those offer continuing education programs more often than degree options.

That's one reason why marketing isn't yet a specialized business profession in Japan – and hence one of several reasons why Japanese companies haven't adopted Western-style market research. But even if formal training in marketing did exist, Japanese executives would probably consider the marketing function too important to leave to mid-level specialists.

Honda is a case in point. When it picked Kihachiro Kawashima to head its U.S. sales organization, the company chose a domestic sales expert who knew very little about the United States. Kawashima ascribes his ultimate success in America to three principles: "Be real, be close to the action, and be localized." What made the difference for Honda in the United States was the senior managers' decision to spend up to 50% of their time visiting and talking with distributors and dealers – the people who knew what U.S. customers really wanted. The ultimate goal of this hands-on, close-to-the-customer approach is to generate a better understanding of customer desires and behavior. The Japanese don't see marketing as something like engineering or finance that can be taught in school. Sensitivity to customers' desires is learned through hard work and experience.

Consensus decision making. In contrast to Western practice, Japanese executives don't give managers sole responsibility for a research area. They conduct research and make decisions by consensus, and they lean toward their intuitive judgment. Rarely do Japanese executives call in an outside professional, and when they do, they often disregard the consultant's report if it goes against their instincts about the best course of action. When Kozo Ohsone, the executive in charge of developing Sony's portable, compact Discman, heard that the company's marketing people were thinking about commissioning a research study, he told them not to waste their money.

Lack of diversification. Tight channel monitoring is also closely associated with the more specialized nature of Japanese industry. Most Japanese corporations have only one or a few related product lines, so managers and employees at all levels can learn more easily what's needed to succeed in the business. This specialization fosters an inductive, bottom-up approach to business planning and problem solving, whereas U.S. and European managements favor more deductive, top-down planning methods. Many large, diversified American corporations have to depend on Western-style market research because they lack the experience and knowledge to sell effectively in multiple industries. But outside marketing consultants and the battery of survey and other research tools they offer cannot fully substitute for intimate knowledge of distribution channels and customer tastes.

But will it be enough?

General Electric's chief, John F. Welch, put it this way, "The Japanese have got the American consumer's number." Hands-on market research has given Japanese companies solid beachheads in the United States and other countries. Especially in mature industries like consumer goods, where customer preferences are so well understood, incremental adjustments in product features or promotional tactics may be all that is needed to have a competitive product.

Japanese-style research is starting to catch on in the United States and in other Western countries. Western executives are trying to get close to the customer and fine-tune product lines and marketing practices after listening carefully to what customers and distributors tell them. But this practice is still the exception in the West.

Ironically, just as some American and European executives are adopting a hands-on approach, a few Japanese companies are asking if their market research style can sustain their competitive edge over the long run—especially in the global marketplace. Some Canon executives, for example, are coming around to the view that surveys and other more scientific methods may be necessary as the company begins to look for ways to diversify.

Why are both sides changing like this? Increasing internationalization of both industries and business practices is doubtless one important reason. Global marketing is leading to a blending of managerial cultures and practices for all countries. Japanese executives are now thinking they may need some Western practices to keep their overseas footholds.

Consider, for example, the problem that Shiseido experienced in the U.S. market. Because it followed the Japanese tradition of sending in executives and managers from the home country, rather than hiring foreign nationals to fill top overseas posts, the company made no headway in the United States for ten years. No one at Shiseido headquarters understood that its cosmetics had to be introduced first into the high-status New York City stores before they could be sold successfully elsewhere. Only after hiring an experienced American cosmetics executive did Shiseido finally get its U.S. marketing effort on the right track.

Japanese corporations' reluctance to hire non-Japanese executives reflects a kind of provincialism that now poses hazards in an era of global markets. Their approach to market research could reinforce this parochialism because it focuses management attention on products and markets that the company already knows well—rather than on potential markets and industries. In their intensive channel monitoring, Japanese business leaders may see only narrow paths and miss the big picture.

Japanese executives today may need a broader perspective than they have taken in the past. Concentration on step-by-step marketing changes may keep them from spotting the social and economic trends that can throw seemingly unshakable industries into upheaval—precisely the changes that large-scale surveys and other Western-style methods uncover very effectively. As bulging surplus cash reserves and global marketing pressures push big Japanese corporations to diversify, more Japanese managers may begin to consider the potential advantages of Western-style market research.

Reprint 87303

When, where, and how to test market

From a leading company's experience, here are practical lessons about the uses and limitations of an extremely important tool in marketing

N.D. Cadbury

The decision to test market a new product should never be routine. Test marketing is costly, laborious, and time consuming; often the information desired can be obtained more efficiently by product research. Nevertheless, the experience of Cadbury Limited, the well-known British producer of confectionery and grocery products, shows that test marketing may be invaluable for forecasting demand, indicating the probable source and quality of sales, as well as what volume of sales can be anticipated. In this article, Cadbury's experience is analyzed for guidelines on how to measure the results of test marketing, how to select regions for testing, how long to make the test period, and other important decisions. The company has also learned useful lessons about why some new products fail in spite of test marketing. The terms *test marketing* (used in the United Kingdom) and *market testing* (U.S. phraseology) describe all types of marketing experimentation. Both terms mean the same thing and include the testing of new products; changes in existing products; alterations to the weight of advertising and its execution; and variations of price, package design, and product recipe. In this article, "test marketing" and "test launching" refer only to the testing of new products and do not embrace the testing of changes in established products or experimenting with their mix of marketing support.

Mr. Cadbury is chairman of Cadbury Typhoo Limited. He was formerly associated with the company's Confectionery Group as marketing director and is a director of the parent company, Cadbury Schweppes Limited.

Test markets are an established part of marketing folklore and an accepted piece of the marketing armory, but do we stop often enough to ask two basic questions: Are these tests always necessary? What circumstances led the company to initiate them?

The relevance of test marketing to an industry depends essentially on the type of manufacturing process involved. The confectionery industry, for example, can frequently produce sufficient quantities of the new product for test market purposes by minor modifications to existing plants and layouts whereas, in the event of a national launch, an entirely new plant may have to be built, which would necessitate a much heavier investment.

Test markets will obviously be inappropriate in industries where the technology requires the same sort of investment for the production of one unit as for a thousand, as in the case of airplanes and cars. No doubt, the British and French governments, for example, and certainly the British and French taxpayers, would have been more enthusiastic about the national commitment to Concorde had they been in a position to test market the prototype in advance.

Consequently, in deciding whether test marketing is a relevant aspect of marketing strategy, the scale of risk and investment implied by the marketing decision must be evaluated. The most visible side of the risk tends to be the cost of plant and machinery that are needed for the new product's manufacture.

But new products also involve other substantial costs: the advertising expenditure; the amount of sales force time occupied by selling the new product; the goodwill and reputation of the company at the wholesale and retail level; the store shelf space required by the new product; and the production and rework problems that always accompany any new line start-up. If test markets enable large parts of these important costs to be deferred until a reliable estimate of national sales can be made, based on actual experience of the product in the marketplace, then test marketing is desirable.

The purpose of this article is to evaluate the uses and limitations of test markets and to describe the role of test marketing within its real context—the field of market research. My premise is that test markets are often employed to discover facts that could just as easily have been established by other cheaper and faster research techniques.

To test or not to test?

Test marketing offers the marketing company two important benefits. First, it provides an opportunity to test a product under typical market conditions in order to obtain a measure of its sales performance. As well as enabling top management to make an accurate prediction of its potential national turnover, this information often forms the basis of the decision whether to extend the product nationally. So the importance of its accuracy is self-evident.

Second, it provides an opportunity, while the product is on limited sale, for management to identify and correct any weaknesses in either the product or its marketing plan before making the commitment to a national sales launch, by which time it will normally be too late—and certainly very expensive—to incorporate product modifications and improvements.

Decision factors

Despite these benefits, however, the decision to test market should never be routine. It is a costly, laborious method of collecting information about reactions to new products, and therefore a test market should be used only as a last resort. The more profitable route to follow with a new product—provided the risk is acceptable and the research sufficiently reassuring—is to launch nationally and avoid the costs and delays of a test market. Test marketing enables the company to minimize losses but not to maximize profits.

There are four major factors that should be considered in determining the efficacy of test marketing:

1
It is necessary to weigh the cost and risk of product failure against the profit and probability of success. For example, at Cadbury Typhoo Limited, though we have test marketed 24 products during the past three years, during this period we have also successfully launched 4 products nationally, but without utilization of a test market phase. In each case of launching nationally, I should stress that the costs and risks of product failure were low.

2
The difference in the scale of investment involved in the test versus national launch route has an important bearing on deciding whether to test. Of the products we have launched directly into national market, very little difference in manufacturing investment was called for whether we opted for a test or national launch. On the one hand, where plant investment for a national launch is considerable, but only slight for a test market, the investment risk favors the test launch approach.

At Cadbury, we have found this to be particularly relevant where, in association with foreign companies, we have been able to import sufficient product to cover test market requirements and so avoid any investment in manufacturing facilities. In the past three years we have test marketed four products that were made by foreign companies in existing plants abroad and that we tested at a price which assumed local production. Now, two of these test markets have provided us with sufficiently encouraging sales performances to justify the planning of local production.

On the other hand, by restricting a product to the test market area during the considerable period required for performance to be predicted accurately, there may be a high opportunity cost. This opportunity cost may amount to the foregone turnover and profit of one year's national sales, depending on how long the product is kept in test.

3
Another factor to be considered is the likelihood and speed with which the competition will be able to copy your product and preempt part of your national

market or overseas markets, should the test be successful. Competitors will be monitoring your test market, and where they have the technology, they will be developing their own versions of your product—and marketing it if you leave the opportunity open for them to do so. Within two years of the start of Cadbury's successful test market of a children's chocolate line (Curly Wurly) in the United Kingdom, we have seen identical competitive versions of the product appear on Canadian, Japanese, West German, and U.S. markets.

4

Apart from the investment in plant and machinery that may be involved, every new product launch is accompanied by a substantial marketing investment that varies with the scale of the launch. New product launches call for heavy advertising and promotional expenditure; they require sales force time, attention, and effort; and they need shelf space in wholesale and retail outlets, which is sometimes obtained only at the expense of the space already given to the company's existing products.

Moreover, if a new product fails, the costs of rebating and reclaiming unwanted stocks from customers have to be faced, along with those costs of writing off unwanted and unusable materials and packaging. Top management should also take into account the possible damage that a new product's failure can inflict on the company: its reputation in the eyes of consumers and customers may be blemished, which is a real if not quantifiable danger.

The foregoing marketing costs—or risks—are reduced by limiting the new product launch to a test market. The cost of concentrating sales force priorities on an unsuccessful new product, and of allowing profitable existing products to lose some share of market as a result, can be greater than the more visible cost of a piece of unwanted machinery.

Our company recently undertook a successful preemptive launch in the soup market. We had identified an opportunity for a powdered snack soup product in the United Kingdom after having observed the success of this product category in other markets, particularly in the United States. Because we had no franchise in the conventional soup market, we faced potential competition from at least four aggressive and highly respected soup manufacturers with strongly established product ranges. Since one of these manufacturers had already test launched a snack soup in the United Kingdom, we realized that the only chance to successfully launch our brand would be to preempt the traditional manufacturers by introducing, distributing, and promoting our brand nationally and being first on the market.

We are currently brand leaders in this segment of the soup market, and an important factor in our success was our recognition that as a nonsoup house we could afford neither the time to test market nor the risk of being swamped by the established competition.

Obviously, there must be some compelling reasons to persuade management of the wisdom of bypassing a test market and moving directly to a national launch. In the case of our entry into the soup market, we felt justified because (a) speed was essential, (b) research had shown the product to be highly acceptable, (c) we judged the package design and advertising to be suitable for the product, and (d) we were involved in only limited manufacturing investment.

Nevertheless, we continue to believe that test marketing is indispensable in order to minimize the major risks involved in most new product launches.

New product research

During the past 10 years our Foods Group has test marketed 13 products, of which 7 have been extended nationally and now account for 33% of that group's turnover. During the past 4 years our Confectionery Group has test marketed 27 products, of which 17 have gone national and will comprise approximately 15% of the company's 1975 confectionery turnover.

I am not suggesting that these success/failure rates are either good or bad or that comparisons with other manufacturers' experience will be meaningful. New product activity and test market performance can only be judged within the total marketing policy and strategy of a particular company and will vary widely between markets and product categories.

To illustrate, confectionery is an indulgent, fun, lighthearted product category, and new product launches provide novelty and variety to sustain consumer interest and create awareness. By contrast, the grocery food market tends to be more conservative, since a nation's eating habits change slowly. This combination probably explains why, for example, the major innovation in the U.K. bread market in the past 20 years has been the sliced variety.

I would only say in assessing our own performance that had we spent more time researching new product candidates, using all the research techniques we now employ, before we made the decision to test market, we could have identified and eliminated a number of failures before the test market stage and so saved ourselves considerable expense and management time.

Before the decision to test market a new product is even considered, we believe that to properly evaluate it, it is important to research all aspects of the product in the form in which it will ultimately be presented to the public. In other words, we want to research not only the product itself but also the name, package design, advertising, and price. The competitive environment that we envisage for the new product is also important in the research.

Using the following total package of research techniques, we are confident that we can expose any major negatives in the package, and either correct them where feasible or abandon the project prior to embarking on the costly test market venture. Here are the steps we follow:

☐
Select a sample of respondents according to their claimed buying habits.
☐
Show respondents the introductory advertising that is planned for the new product and get their reactions to it.
☐
Show the respondents the product and get their pretrial reactions to it.
☐
Give the respondents five samples of the product to test at home.
☐
Conduct an in-home interview to ascertain respondents' (a) posttrial opinions of the product, (b) recall of the advertisement, and (c) claimed intended frequency of purchase.

In addition to these steps, another useful research tool can help to further reduce uncertainty: the model test market. This is a stage of research interposed between pretest research and a full test market. Model test markets simulate the appropriate marketplace in an attempt to reduce both the time necessary to properly evaluate a full test market and the expense involved.

Model test markets are particularly useful in situations where research results have been inconclusive, where considerable capital investment is required to set up even a test market, or where a speedy evaluation of a product's potential is necessary. Model test markets are currently a fashionable area of research development and are becoming increasingly useful as their accuracy and sophistication progress.

The model or mini test market that we use involves a representative panel of housewives who receive a weekly visit at home from a van salesman with a mobile shop. The visit is preceded by the mailing of a sales catalogue and an order form that features the products being tested, along with all the leading brands and any promotional support that is either current or being tested.

There are other types of model test markets but their differences lie in the way the actual marketplace is simulated rather than in what is measured (usually trial, repeat, and frequency of purchase). Since it is the purchasing situation that is simulated, the alternative formats are limited and usually center around different ways to restrict the purchasing of the samples to a medium that the company is able to monitor on an ongoing basis.

Limited capabilities

It would be wrong to suggest that new product research can supply all the answers, or that sales estimates based on the research findings are accurate enough to make the test market stage redundant. A number of factors differentiate research from real-life situations and therefore act as constraints on the degree of predictive accuracy possible prior to gaining test market experience. These factors have to be considered when using the results of research to predict a product's performance.

In research (a) the market in which the new product operates has to be artificially defined and limited, (b) the respondents are acting under enforced 100% trial and repeat trial, and (c) the time factor is artificial, so that management either selects only heavy users of the product or enforces artificially heavy consumption upon lighter users.

Although each new product and test market has its own features, our experience has led us to draw some general conclusions about which product characteristics can be evaluated in research and those which cannot. Specifically, research can indicate the acceptability of recipe, package design, name, price, size, and advertising. But research cannot take the place of a test market when trying to assess the frequency of purchase, novelty value, and extent to which the new product will substitute for sales of existing company products. Also, it cannot indicate the role, character, and position that the product will develop in the minds and purchasing patterns of consumers.

The more unusual or novel the new product, the more difficult it is to assess its future prospects at the research stage. The two most successful products developed by a Cadbury company during the past 20 years have been Smash instant potato and Marvel instant dried skimmed milk. The introduction of these products created quite new markets and caused our competitors to launch similar products.

Yet, when presented with a totally new product concept, respondents cannot predict at the research stage the precise role and position the product will later assume. Smash and Marvel are now regarded by U.K. consumers as universally acceptable and desirable convenience foods. But when they were in the research stage, instant mashed potatoes and skimmed milk evoked memories of wartime substitute foods and images of slothful housewives looking for the easy way out, not taking the time and trouble to prepare the real thing for their families. The marketing success and brand acceptance later achieved by these products could never have been forecast from research alone. Research could not indicate that the two brands would totally alter consumers' perceptions of the product categories.

Forecasting the degree of substitution a new product will have from pretest research presupposes a level of knowledge of consumer behavior in the marketplace that marketing managers do not yet possess. The only accurate way of assessing substitution is through a test market. This need was an important factor in our determining recently to launch a second premium-priced liquer-flavored chocolate bar. We had developed the market ourselves with a rum and raisin chocolate bar two years before. Thus there was no benefit to Cadbury in launching the second product unless it successfully expanded the total market, not simply leaving the company with the same market shared by two products.

In a test market we were able to show that the degree of substitution could be kept to an acceptable level. This was subsequently verified when more than 50% of the new product's sales came from market expansion.

In a highly developed and saturated market like confectionery, new products seldom increase overall consumer consumption, so to be successful they have to reduce sales of existing products. It follows then that a confectionery manufacturer needs to satisfy himself as far as possible that his proposed launch will substitute for his competitors' products rather than for his own.

Measuring test performance

To assess performance in the test market, management needs to know not just the volume of sales, but also the nature of those sales: where they are coming from, and what levels of retail distribution are being achieved.

It is necessary to agree on standards or targets for all these factors before commencement of the test market. The real difficulty of this is the way these standards vary between products and markets. Nevertheless, a manufacturer ought to know his markets, and through the establishment of norms he ought eventually to be able to determine satisfactory criteria with which to measure his test market performance. At Cadbury, we have well-defined objectives for test markets that relate to volume of sales, trial, repeat, and frequency of purchase, distribution, and brand share (where appropriate).

Important criteria

The sales budget or target in the experimental region will be directly related to the level of national turnover that would justify a national extension of the new product. Performance against the sales budget can be measured simply and regularly from the weekly sales receipts. There is always the danger that the sales total in the experimental region will be inflated by exporting to other regions. While this cannot be prevented altogether, it should be kept to a minimum. Otherwise an inflated assessment of test market performance will occur.

The source of sale is important in indicating the future level of settled-down sale. To assess the source, we audit the experimental region every two months after launch to check consumer awareness, trial, and repeat purchase of the product. This audit reveals whether the advertising is motivating people to try the product, and—most important—whether having tried the product, they buy it again.

The repeat purchase figure is the key to the level of settled-down sale. If the product does not match the consumer expectation created by the advertising and presentation, repeat sales will be disappointing even though early test market results have indicated success.

For this reason there should not be too much dependence on the results observed during the early days of a test market. High sales reflect high trial purchases, while a low initial takeoff may simply signal that the advertising lacks impact, something which can usually be corrected during the test. Satisfactory settled-down sale will only be achieved if a large enough core of regular purchasers can be gained for the product, and naturally, this will not be apparent during the early stages of the test market.

It is important to establish what share of the market a new product is acquiring so as to assess its relative performance and to confirm the size of the market being competed for. With a product named Cheers, we overestimated the market for cold milk additives in the United Kingdom by assuming that the growth observed before our launch would continue. In fact, it did not. The market leveled off, and our volume expectation for the product was, with the benefit of hindsight, unrealistic. Our mistake had been to overestimate the future size of the market sector into which we were launching.

Currently, through subscribing to a retail audit every two months, we are able to monitor market share performance, market sizes and trends, and—within that framework—the performance of our own product in terms of share, shop and sterling distribution, purchasing distribution, sales per point of sterling distribution, retailer purchases, consumer sales, and stock cover. "Shop" distribution, expressed as a percentage of the total number of potential stockists, is the number of shops stocking a product; "sterling" distribution measures the share of total retail sales held by those retailers stocking the product. So, if Brand X is in 50% of grocery outlets and those outlets have 75% of total grocery sales, Brand X will be described as having 50% "shop" and 75% "sterling" distribution. For the United States, simply read "dollar" for "sterling."

The foregoing combination of data can be extremely useful in tracking the development of the new brand and in identifying problem areas associated with it. In addition, special analyses can be helpful in pinpointing marketing problems associated with, for example, age of stocks, cumulative distribution, pricing, display, and merchandising.

Incidentally, the action standard we set for new grocery products in terms of sterling distribution is 65% nationally, but this standard will vary among product categories.

As I have already indicated, our leading share of the confectionery market means that we are vitally concerned with the substitution or cannibalization factor any proposed new confectionery product will have on our existing range. The objective of our new product program is to win share from our competitors. Thus to judge the value of a new product, we need to measure the performance of existing products (our own and competitors') in order to assess whether the new product sales are coming from ourselves or the competition. The results here can have an important bearing on management's final judgment of the test market.

Distribution targets for major categories of potential stocklists are agreed on in advance with sales force management. These targets must be realistic if they are to have sales force commitment. And so we set them to peak after 12 months. The time it takes to achieve full distribution will depend on the size and effectiveness of the company sales force, and on the nature of the particular market's wholesale and retail distribution pipelines.

Selection of test region

Since more than 90% of Cadbury's media expenditure is on television, the eight TV boundaries in the United Kingdom determine our test regions. None of these regions conforms to the national pattern of food and confectionery consumption and expenditure. Because we cannot pick a representative region, the important thing for us to know is by how much each region varies from the national pattern. With this knowledge we can develop a behavioral factor for each region that we can consider when extrapolating national sales. Our experience shows that when differences in purchasing patterns between regions are neglected, an error of more than 50% can result—certainly sufficient to present a quite inaccurate picture of subsequent national outcome.

While we have not used two test regions for the same product, such a course would provide more evidence on which to base final predictions, though it would involve increased marketing, and possibly production, investment. The use of two test regions could be a particularly appropriate route were it intended to test two quite different marketing strategies for the same product (e.g., aiming the product exclusively at children in one region and at mothers for their children in another).

In summary, our choice of test region is governed by logistics rather than the individual characteristics of any region. The determination of our final decision is based on factors such as our own existing marketing activity, that of competitors, availability of stock, seasonality, the size of the test area in relation to the budget set for the product, the structure of the trade in the selected area, and the degree of anticipated retailer cooperation.

Control of experimental market

Care must be taken to avoid distortions in test market results. The conditions in the experimental region, for example, should resemble as nearly as possible those under which the product would be launched nationally. Even though any new product should receive priority from the sales force and intensive marketing support during the launch period, the support in the test area must be of the same weight as could be afforded on a national basis. In spite of the natural temptation for marketing managers to seek disproportionate attention to sales and marketing support for their test launches, such temptation has to be resisted: the research or forecasting manager must make an objective prediction that assumes normal support.

While top management can control the company's activity in the experimental area, competitive activity unfortunately cannot be so regulated. The important thing is to allow for any unusual competitive activity when assessing test market results.

Exhibit I
Levels of distribution achieved for two new confectionery products

Months after launch	2	4	6	8	10	12
Percentage of outlets stocking products:						
Success	32	61	69	72	78	80
Failure	32	59	60	59	60	55

Other distortions may be caused during the test market by stock shortages of the test or competing products, or by modifications made during the test to the product or its marketing plan. It is consequently important that the test market run long enough so that the effects of these distortions and changes will either have disappeared or made their full impact on the level of settled-down sale.

Length of test run

One question frequently asked is: How long should a test market run? The answer will depend on the length of time it takes to judge the product's performance against the company's objectives for it. Time must be allowed for sales to settle down from their initial honeymoon level; in addition, the share and sales levels must be allowed to stabilize. After the introduction of a product, peaks and troughs will inevitably stem from initial consumer interest and curiosity—as well as from competitive product retaliation.

Sufficient time should be given to iron out any deficiencies in either the product or the marketing program. If the advertising is not communicating, then new advertising will have to be developed and implemented if the product is to be given a proper trial. If the package design lacks impact, this too can probably be corrected during the test.

Time must also be allowed for planned levels of distribution to be achieved. To illustrate, *Exhibit I* gives the distribution figures reached during test market by two new Cadbury confectionery products. One was subsequently judged successful and was therefore extended; the other failed to meet the criteria laid down and was later withdrawn.

The reader can see that at least for the first six months there is no appreciable difference in the relative levels of distribution achieved, but thereafter distribution of the unsuccessful product begins to tail off. While some clear success and failure can be identified sooner, we place little weight on test market results achieved during the first six months. After that, the pattern of repeat sales begins to establish itself and accurate predictions become possible.

Why products fail

The reasons for new product failure in a test market are normally complex and not easy to identify. A product does not usually fail for one reason alone but rather through a combination of factors. It is nevertheless true that the majority fail because the product does not contain a demonstrable consumer advantage over competitive brands.

An analysis of 18 of our own new product failures reveals the following major reasons for lack of success, together with their relative incidence:

Recipe	7
Conceptual shortcomings	4
Price	3
Package	2
Low volume	2

In the confectionery market as in other food markets, recipe is a key variable and, not surprisingly, it is the most important factor in achieving success or failure. Conceptual shortcomings refer to the overall positioning and advertising of the product. I have not identified advertising as a separate category, because the best advertising execution in the world will not sell a product if it does not meet and satisfy an existing or potential consumer need.

Price determines the value the product offers to consumers, and it is never easy to judge the correct balance between profitability and the need to be competitive. Nevertheless, there is no purpose in test marketing new products at a price that will not meet the company's profit objectives. Thus the argument that a new product must be launched at a price below the competition is a dangerous one, because it simply delays the time when the product must be priced to produce satisfactory profits. If a product meets a need, consumers will pay for it.

The package (i.e., its size, composition, and design) is another criterion that plays a key part in determining the acceptability, visibility, and impact of a new product in the marketplace.

Illustrative failures

Here are four examples of mistakes we made that resulted in favorable research findings but led nevertheless to new product failure in the test market:

1
In the case of a new biscuit product, we were never able to match in commercial production the product samples which had been made up in the R&D laboratory for the research tests. The product we test marketed was neither the same nor as good as the product we initially developed, and the sales in the test market never came up to expectation. The lesson is a simple one: be sure you are researching with samples identical to the product you plan to market.

2
As a result of our success with Smash instant potato, we developed an instant croquette potato under the brand name Smasher. Our home economics unit had prepared the samples in shallow pans during research sessions, and housewives had not given any indication that they would have difficulty making up the finished product.

However, it turned out that the majority of housewives did not possess the appropriate shallow pans that our well-equipped home economics unit had been using, and the product was very difficult to prepare in the deeper saucepans found in most British kitchens. Therefore, despite the good rating the product itself had received, difficulty of preparation torpedoed it.

3
We developed a fresh cream product called Swiss Dessert, which received excellent ratings from consumers in research. The product was tetra packaged, which preserved the potentially unstable dessert safely, but the new package was impossible to stack and difficult to display. Thus it proved to be unpopular with the grocery trade and never received adequate support in the test market area.

4
We developed an instant tea under the brand name Fine Brew, which—prior to the advent of the tea bag—had important convenience advantages over the

conventional pot-brewing ritual. The product researched well and we proceeded into test market, where the product proved singularly unsuccessful. The concentration of the tea was so strong that half a teaspoon was sufficient per cup, and so small a measure made preparation difficult. It is also possible that we underestimated the challenge of weaning the British public from the traditional teapot.

Future developments

Marketing companies will only improve their test market strike rate and predictive accuracy when they develop ways of more accurately identifying and recognizing the characteristics of consumer behavior and patterns of consumer expenditure which shape our markets month by month. Marketing knowledge in this area is inadequate.

Thus the need for test marketing in the future will be primarily governed by developments in marketing knowledge and understanding of the mechanics of consumer behavior. The better top management understands its markets, the less frequently will test markets fail, and the sooner it will be able to risk dispensing with test markets altogether.

At Cadbury we are learning much from the correlation of pretest market research data with the launch sales patterns which subsequently develop. This information is revealing identifiable differences between the brands that succeed and those that fail in test market. If successful and unsuccessful patterns can be established and recognized at the pretest stage, we will not only be able to abandon at an earlier stage the projects likely to fail, but perhaps we can also reach the point where the test marketing of new products becomes redundant.

However, that day is a long way off, and our research techniques—whether they consist of total package tests, extended in-home placement tests, mobile shops, or controlled warehouses—will all have to be developed considerably before an acceptable substitute for test marketing can be claimed.

Of equal significance to future developments is the use and analysis of consumer panel data. These data give us a record of consumer purchasing and consumption behavior, and they can be enormously valuable in providing information from which we can learn how consumers do in fact behave. Most definitions of markets are manufacturer-oriented and relate to sales of the product rather than to the consumer who makes the buying decision. For example, we talk of the boxed chocolate assortment market, when boxes of chocolate are also competing in the consumer's mind with flowers, records, books, and other semicasual gifts.

Market definition can have an important bearing on the way consumer research of a new product is structured. We need to know which consumers are potential purchasers of our brands, how many of them there are, how frequently they buy and switch brands, which other brands they buy, and how best we can communicate to them. If we knew more about our consumers and their buying behavior, we could make our test market, and marketing activity generally, more accurate and less wasteful.

Meanwhile, there is a knowledge gap between pretest market research and the national launch, and for now it can be bridged only by the test market. Though existing research techniques are useful, none can replicate the market situation, and this is the unique contribution of the test market. For this reason test marketing will continue to be a most important marketing tool and gatherer of information for marketing decision making.

Reprint 75303

HBR CASE STUDY

The Case of the Test Market Toss-up

Should Paradise Foods put its new frozen dessert on ice?

by Steven H. Star and Glen L. Urban

Bill Horton sat alone in his office late Friday afternoon anxiously leafing through computer printouts, even though he could recite their contents from memory. Horton was waiting for his boss, Bob Murphy, to report back the decision on a subject the marketing committee had been debating for more than four hours. The issue—whether Paradise Foods should authorize national rollout of a new product, Sweet Dream, to complement its established frozen specialty dessert, LaTreat. Horton was product manager for Sweet Dream, and Murphy was the group manager responsible for all new products in Paradise's dessert line.

"I'm glad you're sitting," Bob quipped uncomfortably as he entered Bill's office. "The news isn't good. The committee decided not to go ahead."

Steven H. Star is director of the marketing center at MIT's Sloan School of Management. Glen L. Urban is Dai-Ichi Kangyo Bank Professor of Management and deputy dean of the Sloan School. Their book, Advanced Marketing Management: Strategic Analysis and Decisions, *will be published next year.*

"I don't believe it," Bill protested. "I started to worry when the meeting dragged on, but I never thought they'd say no. Damn. Eighteen months down the drain."

"I know how you feel, but you have to understand where the committee was coming from. It was a real close call—as close as I can remember since I've had this job. But the more carefully they considered your

Why launch Sweet Dream if it steals share from LaTreat?

test results, the more it looked like the returns just weren't there."

"Not there? All they had to look at was Appendix B in my report—the data from Midland and Pittsfield. Sweet Dream got a 3% share after 26 weeks. A trial rate of 15%. A repurchase rate of 45%. If national performance were anywhere close to that, we'd have our launch costs back in 14 months. Who can argue with that?"

"I'm on your side here, but I only had one vote," Bob said defensively. "We both knew what Barbara's position was going to be—and you know how much weight she carries around here these days." Barbara Mayer was the Paradise group manager responsible for established dessert products. She became a "grouper" in 1985, after two enormously successful years as LaTreat's first product manager.

"And to be honest, it was tough to take issue with her," Bob continued. "What's the point of introducing Sweet Dream if you end up stealing share from LaTreat? In fact, Barbara used some of *your* data against us. She kept waving around Appendix C, griping that 75% of the people who tried Sweet Dream had bought LaTreat in the previous four weeks. And repurchase rates were highest among LaTreat heavy users. You know how the fourteenth floor feels about LaTreat. Barbara claims that adjusting for lost LaTreat sales means Sweet Dream doesn't recover its up-front costs for three years."

Launched in 1983, LaTreat was the first "super premium" frozen dessert to enter national distribution. It consisted of 3.5 ounces of vanilla ice cream dipped in penuche fudge and covered with almonds. An individual bar sold for just under $2 and a package of four was $7. Unlike LaTreat, which came on a stick, Sweet Dream resembled an ice cream sandwich. It consisted of sweet-cream ice cream between two oversized chocolate chip cookies and coated with dark Belgian chocolate. Its price was comparable to LaTreat's.

Under Barbara Mayer, annual sales of LaTreat soon reached $40 million, and it began making a significant contribution to dessert group profits. It accounted for almost 5% of the market despite a price about 50% higher than standard frozen specialties. Lately, however, competition had stiffened. LaTreat faced tough challenges from three direct competitors as well as several parallel concepts (like Sweet Dream) at various stages of test marketing. The total frozen specialties market had grown fast enough to absorb these new entrants without reducing LaTreat sales, but revenues had been essentially flat through 1986 and 1987.

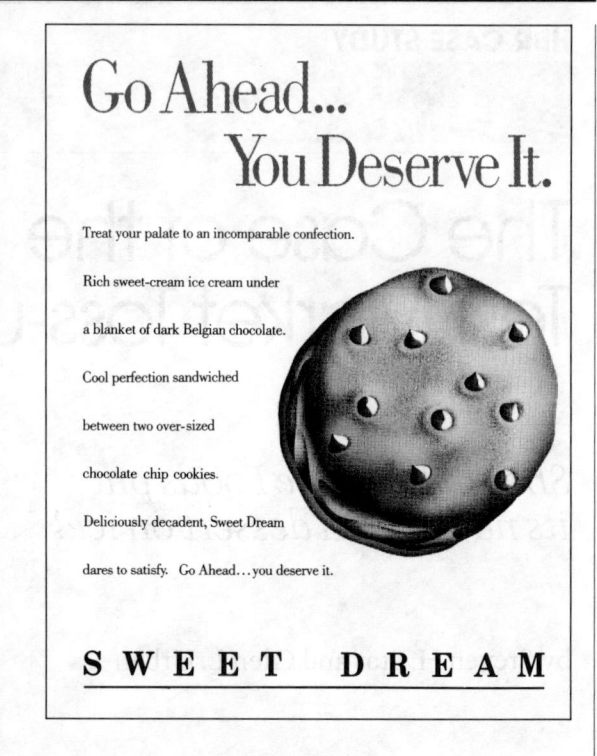

Bill understood the importance of LaTreat, but he was not the type to mince words. "You and I both know things are more complicated than Barbara would have people believe," he told Bob. "There wasn't the same cannibalization effect in Marion and Corvallis. And we never did a test in Midland and Pittsfield where Barbara's people were free to defend La-Treat. We might be able to have it both ways..."

Bob interrupted. "Bill, we could stay here all night on this. But what's the point? The committee's made its decision. You don't like it, I don't like it. But these aren't stupid people. It's hard to argue with the dessert group's batting average over the last five years. This may ring hollow right now, but you can't take this personally."

"That's easy for you to say," Bill sighed.

"You know how this company works," Bob reminded him. "We don't hold withdrawal of a new product against the manager if withdrawal is the right decision. Hell, it happened to me ten years ago with that dumb strawberry topping. It made sense to kill that product. And I was better off at the company for it. The fact is, the committee was impressed as hell with the research you did—although to be honest, you may have overwhelmed them. A 40-page report with 30 pages of appendixes. I had trouble wading through it all. But that doesn't matter. You did a great job, and the people who count know that."

"I appreciate the sentiment, but that's not why I think this is the wrong decision. Sweet Dream is a go on the merits."

"Go home, play some golf this weekend," Bob counseled. "Things won't seem so bleak on Monday."

Bill never made it to the country club. Instead, he spent the weekend worrying about his future at Paradise and puzzling over how the marketing committee could have reached its no-launch decision.

Paradise Foods was a large, successful manufacturer of packaged foods and household products whose markets were becoming increasingly competitive. Bill believed that Paradise was vulnerable in this treacherous environment because of its failure to keep pace with technological change—in particular, the increasing sophistication of marketing research based on computer modeling, supermarket scanner data, and targetable cable television. Paradise certainly used these tools, but to Bill's way of thinking, top management didn't embrace them with the same enthusiasm as other companies.

When Bill became product manager for Sweet Dream, he promised himself he would do a state-of-the-art research job. The plan was to compare the performance of Sweet Dream in two test markets exposed to different advertising and promotion strategies. The campaign in Midland, Texas and Pittsfield, Massachusetts struck an overtly self-indulgent tone—"Go Ahead, You Deserve It"—and used limited price promotion to induce trial. The campaign in Marion, Indiana and Corvallis, Oregon emphasized superior quality—"Taste the Goodness"—and used promotion aggressively. Sunday newspapers in the two cities frequently carried 50-cents-off coupons, and Sweet Dream boxes included a 75-cent rebate voucher.

Bill used two computer-based research services—InfoScan and BehaviorScan—to evaluate Sweet Dream's performance and long-term potential.[1] InfoScan tracks product purchases on a national and local basis for the packaged-goods industry. It collects point-of-sale information on all bar-coded products sold in a representative sample of supermarkets and drugstores. It generates weekly data on volume, price, mar-

---

1. InfoScan® and BehaviorScan® are actual services offered by Information Resources, Inc.

ket share, the relationship between sales and promotional offers, and merchandising conditions. Bill subscribed to InfoScan to monitor competitive trends in the frozen specialties segment.

BehaviorScan is used in marketing tests to measure the effect of marketing strategies on product purchases. In a typical BehaviorScan test, one group of consumer panel-

Bill's research generated a stack of computer printouts. But what do the numbers mean?

ists is exposed to certain variables (i.e., print or television advertisements, coupons, free samples, in-store displays), while other participating consumers serve as a control group. Company analysts use supermarket scanner data on both groups of consumers (who present identification cards to store checkout clerks) to evaluate purchasing responses to marketing campaigns. A typical BehaviorScan test lasts about one year.

Bill Horton's research program had generated a stack of computer printouts several feet high. He had spent much of the spring trying to unravel the complex interactions between different advertising and promotion strategies for Sweet Dream, the various promotion deals Paradise was running on LaTreat, and the proliferation of other frozen specialties. Despite Bob's advice to relax, Bill spent Sunday afternoon in front of his home computer, massaging the data one last time.

On Monday, Bill arrived at his office a few minutes late. He was surprised to find Barbara Mayer waiting for him.

"Sorry to drop in on you first thing," she said, "but I wanted to let you know what a fantastic job you did on the Sweet Dream test. I'm sure you were disappointed with the committee's decision, and in a way I was too. It would have been great to work together on the rollout. But the data were pretty clear. We didn't have a choice."

"Well, I thought the data were clear too – but in the opposite direction."

"Come on, Bill, you can understand the logic of the decision. The Midland and Pittsfield numbers were fine, but they were coming at the expense of LaTreat. There wasn't so much cannibalization in Marion and Corvallis, but the Sweet Dream numbers weren't as good either. Trial was acceptable, but repurchase was low. We might make money, but we'd never meet the hurdle rate. Every so often a product just falls between two stools."

"So we'll do more tests," Bill countered. "We can play with the positioning in Marion and Corvallis. Or we can start from scratch somewhere else. I can have us wired to go in three weeks."

"We've already taken 18 months on Sweet Dream," Barbara said. "The committee felt it was time to try new concepts. I don't think that's so unreasonable."

"You're forgetting two things," Bill replied. "First, with freezer space as tight as it is, the longer it takes to come up with another product, the harder the stores are going to squeeze us. Second, other people are going to find out how well Sweet Dream did in Midland and Pittsfield. We're the only ones who get the BehaviorScan numbers, but you know the competition is monitoring our tests. What do you think Weston & Williams is going to do when it sees the results? It'll have a Sweet Dream clone out in a few months if we don't launch."

Weston & Williams (W&W) was a leading supplier of household products that was diversifying into foods, including desserts. It had a reputation as a conservative company that insisted on exhaustive prelaunch research. But the trade press recently had reported on W&W's decision to rush Pounce – a combination detergent, colorfast bleach, and fabric softener – to the market on the basis of very preliminary tests and data from a competitor's test markets. W&W had thus become the first national entrant in the "maxiwash" category.

"Bob made that argument Friday," Barbara said. "But you can guess how far he got. The guys upstairs have a tough enough time taking our own computer data seriously. They don't buy the idea that someone else is going to jump into the market based on *our* tests. Plus, that would be a huge risk. Pounce may have given Weston & Williams all the gray hair they can stand for a few years."

"From what I can tell, Barbara, the only issue that counted was cannibalization." Bill's voice betrayed a rekindled sense of frustration. "I understand you want to protect LaTreat. I understand the company wants to protect LaTreat. But it seems to me we're protecting a product that's getting tired."

"What are you talking about?" Barbara objected. "Profits aren't growing as fast as they used to, but they're not dropping either. LaTreat is solid."

"Come on, Barbara. Your people have really been promoting it in the last two quarters – shifting money out of print and TV and into coupons and rebates. Total spending hasn't changed, so profits are OK. But LaTreat has gotten hooked on promotion. And all the wrong kinds of promotion. You've got people accelerating future purchases and price-

Will the competition monitor Sweet Dream's test and launch a clone?

sensitive types jumping in whenever LaTreat goes on sale. Who needs that?"

"Where are you getting this stuff?" Barbara demanded. "I didn't see it in your report."

"I spent the weekend running some more numbers," Bill replied. "Take a look at this."

Bill punched a few buttons on his computer keyboard and called up a series of graphs. The first documented the growing percentage of LaTreat sales connected with promotional offers. A second graph disaggregated LaTreat's promotion-related sales by four buyer categories Bill had created from BehaviorScan data. "Loyalists" were longtime customers who increased their purchases in response to a deal. "Trial users" bought LaTreat for the first time because of the promotion and who seemed to be turning into loyal customers. "Accelerators" were longtime customers who used coupons or rebates to stock up on product they would have bought anyway. "Switch-on-deal" customers were nonusers who bought LaTreat when there were promotions but demonstrated little long-term loyalty. Bill's graph documented that a majority of LaTreat's coupon redeemers fell into the last two categories, with "loyalists" accounting for a shrinking percentage of sales.

Finally, Bill called up his ultimate evidence—a graph that adjusted LaTreat sales to eliminate the effect of promotions. (See the illustration.)

"I'm amazed you spent your weekend doing this," Barbara said, "but I'm glad you did. It'll help us think through future marketing strategies for LaTreat. But it doesn't change what the committee decided. It's time to move on."

"I'm not so sure," Bill replied. "I hope you don't mind, but I think I should show these data to Bob. Maybe he can convince the committee to reconsider. After all, if LaTreat is weakening, it's going to show up in your profit figures sooner or later."

"Data don't make decisions, Bill, people do. And the people on the marketing committee have been in the industry a lot longer than you. Their gut tells them things your computer can't. Besides, you and I both know that when you collect this much data, you can make it show just about anything. Go ahead and talk to Bob, but I'm sure he'll see things the same way I do."

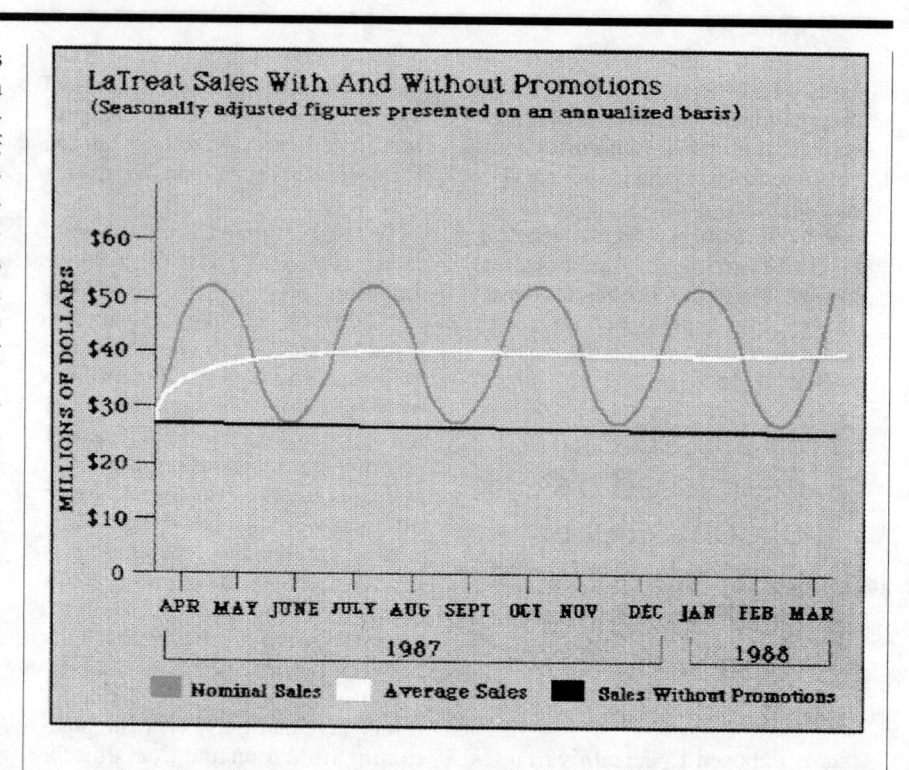

LaTreat Sales With And Without Promotions
(Seasonally adjusted figures presented on an annualized basis)

Nominal Sales   Average Sales   Sales Without Promotions

WHITHER SWEET DREAM?

We asked the following business leaders—a prominent advertising executive, a consultant specializing in market research, and executives from two leading packaged foods companies—to evaluate Bill Horton's performance and to examine whether Paradise Foods should reconsider its no-launch decision.

JERRY DELLA FEMINA *is chairman and CEO of Della Femina, McNamee WCRS, Inc., a New York-based advertising agency whose current clients include Rolls Royce Motor Cars, Sunshine Biscuit Company, and Dow Chemical.*

Keep your cannibals in the family

Bill Horton should quietly—but quickly—look for a new job. His days at Paradise Foods are numbered. Ironically, he won't lose his position because of the "failure" of Sweet Dream. Rather, he'll be a casualty of the austerity moves the dessert group will announce when LaTreat falls out of bed—and fall out of bed it will.

Let's consider life at Paradise Foods nine months or so from now. To the marketing committee, Sweet Dream will be a distant memory. No dessert group executive will utter the word "cannibalization" until it can be used to kill another new product. Barbara Mayer will be thriving in her job despite the surprising emergence of a strong new rival to LaTreat. After all, who could have predicted that a competitor would introduce a frozen specialty dessert, Sweet Fantasy, made of sweet-cream ice cream between two oversized chocolate chip cookies and coated with dark Belgian chocolate? And who could have guessed that Sweet Fantasy would win consumer and trade acceptance as quickly as it did?

Barbara will respond to this urgent threat with the famed "Packaged Goods Grouper's Shuffle." She'll cut radio and television advertising to the bone, increase promotions, and otherwise mortgage LaTreat's future to buy current sales—thereby giving her enough time to move up the Paradise organization chart and leave the mess for her replacement.

Paradise Foods is playing by the marketing rules of 1978 while it does business in 1988. What the marketing committee doesn't seem to realize is that everything in business today is moving at breakneck speed. Sure, Paradise has control over the future of Bill Horton and Sweet Dream. But it has no control over a quick, successful product launch by the competition. Once that happens, executives at Paradise will realize there is something worse than having one part of your company taking a fraction of its sales from another part of your company—and that's letting a competitor walk away with business in a category you've built. In 1988, the rule is: If you must be the victim of a cannibal, make sure the cannibal is a member of your family.

Many years ago, I was part of an exciting success with an imported German white wine. We started with a brand that was selling at about 30,000 cases per year and, in a relatively short time, increased annual volume to 1.2 million cases.

Market research told us some interesting things about this product. It was an entry-level, fruity wine popular among consumers with relatively unsophisticated palates. Our business was like a funnel. Advertising threw consumers into the top of the funnel. They would enjoy our product for a year or so, and come out the bottom looking for a drier wine that better suited their new tastes. That's when they went over to the competition.

So I proposed building a second funnel to stand under the first—a new wine that would be waiting to catch and hold the consumer, perhaps for another year, perhaps even longer. "Cannibalism!" shouted the wine company's executive committee. "What do we need with a second product? We're still growing with our lead product. Let's not cannibalize a good thing. Instead, let's raise our prices."

Alas, there was another funnel built—but it was built by the competition. Today, the company imports 600,000 cases and sales continue to

> **Sweet Dream needs a champion to beat back the Abominable No Men.**

trend down. It hardly advertises anymore, but you can buy its white wine on deal anytime. No one connected with the product can figure out why it failed.

Bill Horton's problems did not start with the decision to abort the Sweet Dream project. They started when he decided to join Paradise Foods. His boss, Bob Murphy, summed up Paradise philosophy on new products when he said, "You know how this company works. We don't hold the withdrawal of a new product against the manager if withdrawal is the right decision."

What's wrong with this generous-sounding sentiment? Everything. A company that excuses new product failures because withdrawal is the "right decision" is sending a message that it is not serious about new products. In all my years in business, covering a wide range of new products, I've never heard anyone say, a year after deciding to abort a new product, that the move was a "bad decision." Memories are short, and few executives are interested in quantifying lost opportunities.

In some companies, aborting product launches is *always* the right decision. In the highly charged and political atmosphere of the Paradise dessert group, people like Barbara (who see another employee's success as a threat to their career) can easily sabotage even the most promising new product. When you add Bob Murphy to the team—an executive to whom status quo is such a religion that he can't possibly be an eloquent voice for new products—the deck is stacked even further against launch.

This is sad because every new product needs a champion in upper management. Someone who will ramrod it past the Abominable No-Men in every company who are just waiting to pounce on anything that's new—be it computer-based marketing research (which is far more reliable than their "guts" ever were), or a marketing idea that would signal that their company is living in the present rather than in the much-overrated "good ol' days."

I can sympathize with Bill. I've worked with a few companies who paid lip service to new product programs. These companies are masters at something I call "new product foreplay." They titillate themselves and their employees, but rarely deliver anything.

I've also been fortunate enough to work with companies that see new products for what they are—their future—and are relentless in their desire to develop and successfully market as many as they can. One such company, which makes air fresheners, is the antithesis of Paradise. It's the kind of company where Bill Horton would thrive.

Like Paradise, the air freshener company had a successful product (a carpet deodorizer) that was called "the number one new product introduction in the household category" the year it was introduced. When reports of the product's success started rolling in, management immediately looked for further opportunities in that product area to fend off the competition they knew would soon be coming straight at them.

At my agency, we played a marketing war game to anticipate the competition's moves. I selected three executives who had experience working with our client's largest potential competitors. I assigned each of them to a different competitor and gave them the same job. "You are a group product manager. You're sitting at your desk when your boss comes in with this new carpet deodorizer and says, 'This product is going through the roof. I want us to have a product out in the next nine months. Give me your marketing plan for it.'"

Our first competitor had a long and distinguished new product record, but it had never brought out a new product in less than three years. We decided to ignore it. The second company had a history of developing whole lines of new products. We were sure it would come out with as many different fragrances of carpet freshener as it could. It did. We also thought this strategy would fail. It did.

The third company was the one we worried most about. It had a track record of coming to market within six months after the introduction of a successful new product. It was essentially a knockoff company. We figured it would market a carpet freshener that was not as good as ours, but would price it considerably lower, not back it with an advertising program, and come out dealing.

We decided that if there was going to be cannibalization, we were going to be our own cannibals. So we knocked off our own product and brought it out at a price a few cents below what we determined our competitor would offer. We introduced the product four months after the appearance of the first carpet freshener and succeeded in taking valuable shelf space from our competitor. We used a quick, highly visible advertising launch and then cut the budget to nothing.

Our war plan worked. The new product introduction discouraged our competitor from even trying to enter the business. Had the Paradise marketing committee applied this same philosophy to LaTreat, Sweet Dream would be a success instead of an expensive bad memory. Bill Horton would be happy, Barbara Mayer would learn to live with internal competition, Bob Murphy would learn that it takes courage (not goodwill) to develop new products, and Paradise would be just that for its employees and stockholders.

WILLIAM H. MOULT *is executive vice president of Cincinnati-based SAMI/Burke, the world's second largest marketing research firm.*

It takes a pro to use power tools

Would a heart patient visit a cardiologist merely to get access to an EKG monitor? Would you drive your sports car to a highly regarded repair shop just to borrow a wrench? What most disturbs me about how Paradise Foods has approached the Sweet Dream launch is that senior management made no attempt to ensure that marketing research techniques were used appropriately and effectively.

Supermarket scanners, electronic test market facilities, and computer-based marketing models are the new power tools of the packaged goods industry. The product data available today are vastly richer than that which were available even five years ago, and the computer models used to analyze the data are much more robust. It's easy for companies to get access to mountains of data and complicated models. It's much more difficult to interpret the data with the necessary sophistication and caution.

That's certainly true of Bill Horton, who made several big mistakes during his research on Sweet Dream. Bill exhibited some admirable qualities—going so far as to risk his golf handicap by spending his weekend glued to a computer screen. But even the most talented new product managers often lack (perhaps by design) at least three of the ingredients that are essential to making a sound decision in a case like the Sweet Dream launch: (1) objectivity, (2) the perspective that comes from having wrestled with many previous launches, (3) experience in applying complex research and analytical methods.

Most large packaged goods companies have highly qualified marketing researchers on their staffs. Companies that don't have veteran in-house researchers can and should demand analytical support from their marketing research suppliers. There are only a few companies that provide services like electronic test markets, scanner panel data bases, and validated marketing models. But it's precisely these companies that have attracted many of the industry's best analysts. Using them merely to provide raw data or access to market testing facilities is getting bad value for the money.

I propose adding a new character to this case, who I'll call Joe. Joe is a test marketing analyst with a good deal of experience in new product launches. What issues would this veteran analyst raise in evaluating Sweet Dream that Bill Horton overlooked?

First, Joe would design his research program after having consulted closely with the senior managers at Paradise responsible for the rollout decision. With a little luck and an enlightened client, everyone would agree that launching Sweet Dream is not the only risk Paradise faces. The real issue is the fate of its entire frozen specialities line. Indeed, a well-executed launch may *reduce* the larger risks to Paradise's presence in a market segment subject to intense and increasing brand competition. So there are essentially two options on the table: LaTreat alone, and LaTreat plus Sweet Dream.

Any marketing analyst with experience in the 1980s has grappled numerous times with such proposed line extensions. Joe would immediately anticipate the concerns about cannibalization and structure his research accordingly. For example, he would develop a state-of-the-art "source of volume" model that allows him to understand, with a good deal of confidence, where Sweet Dream's sales are coming from. Is the new product drawing directly from other frozen specialties? Is it attracting new consumers to increase overall frozen-specialty purchases, thereby mitigating the cannibalization threat? These are the questions to which the marketing committee wants hard answers—questions that Bill Horton can answer only indirectly.

Joe's second major challenge is to forecast Sweet Dream's postlaunch performance based on the test market results and Paradise's agenda for the product. (The rollout might be nationwide, or the company might want to introduce the product on a regional basis.) Even if Joe is one of the industry's most gifted analysts, his palms are a bit sweaty when he delivers the forecast. Extrapolating from test markets is a notoriously tricky undertaking. But Joe understands these complexities, and he will be sure to avoid the classic pitfalls.

One set of pitfalls involves what I call the "tender loving care" and "forced distribution" effects. In a segment as competitive as frozen desserts, is it realistic to expect Sweet Dream to get as much freezer space nationwide as it did in the test supermarkets? Will the product be displayed as aggressively? Will Paradise's sales force and distributors pay as much attention to it? The likely answers to these questions are no. Joe might go so far as to suggest starting the Sweet Dream launch with a "sell-in" test in a lead market to verify that Paradise will be able to deliver on the company's retail stocking objectives.

There are also certain analyses Joe would avoid. For example, he would recognize that running a model to "de-promote" LaTreat while ignoring the long-term implications of such a policy would be a bit like do-it-yourself brain surgery in the hands of the uninitiated. The data Bill calls up on his computer screen to confront Barbara is at best a first cut at understanding the relationship between promotion and the strength of the LaTreat franchise. In a category as hotly contested as frozen specialties, regular and heavy promotion may be the only way to maintain even a rock-solid brand.

Joe's final presentation to the marketing committee would be as short or as long as Paradise management culture might require—but he wouldn't even think about subjecting senior managers to a 40-page report with a 30-page appendix. He would also stress that his research and market models do not replace sound executive judgment. Research information is merely a foundation on which to build that judgment.

Overall, the case for launching Sweet Dream seems compelling. A repurchase rate of 45% after 26 weeks is impressively high by industry standards. Indeed, it represents high enough consumer satisfaction that this product may be worth fighting for—even if it means flexibility on Paradise's short-term hurdle rate in favor of Sweet Dream's long-term potential. With good execution, Paradise may effectively close important potential competitors out of the limited freezer space available for this high-margin segment. If so, the company could enjoy the lion's share of the benefits from continued category growth.

Data dumps and a stifling organization

Bill Horton has all the data he needs to support the launch of Sweet Dream. Indeed, he seems to have *too much* data in terms of how he has packaged it for the marketing committee. One can only speculate about what Bill chose to include in his 40-page report and 30-page appendix, but he failed to persuade a group of managers skeptical of computer printouts in the first place.

JOHN M. KEENAN *is executive vice president of General Foods Worldwide in Rye Brook, New York. He joined the company 25 years ago as an assistant product manager in the Jell-O division.*

Moreover, he failed to include some key consumer buying data on LaTreat.

His appendix sounds like what I call a "data dump"—reams of computer-generated information designed to impress by weight rather than by keen insights presented in a form familiar and comfortable to executives who did not grow up with terminals on their desks. I find it equally frustrating when researchers simply share the output of a computer model ("this new product will have a 15% internal rate of return") without explaining the model's central assumptions and inputs—background that allows senior managers to bring their experience and judgment to bear on the computer-generated results.

Why should Paradise launch Sweet Dream?

1. LaTreat is an older product in a category that thrives on novelty.

> **Too often, new products lose the close calls to established cash cows.**

Bill's breakdown of LaTreat sales by customer categories is compelling evidence that there is plenty of room for a new premium-priced, indulgent dessert. LaTreat will suffer cannibalization from competitive entries if not from Sweet Dream.

2. Sweet Dream should be able to cannibalize LaTreat at a favorable absolute contribution margin level. That is, overall dessert-group profits will increase by having both products on supermarket shelves. Sweet Dream has done well in its low promotion markets (Midland and Pittsfield) while more aggressive promotion in Corvallis and Marion simply generated a lower quality trial by price shoppers—hence the lower repeat rate. Paradise needs a coordinated strategy for its two products that will maximize their combined profits.

3. In the Sweet Dream rollout, LaTreat will be able to defend its hardcore users. This should improve total company share of the frozen specialties category and reduce the three-year payout period that Barbara Mayer calculated for the marketing committee.

While Bill could have done a better job organizing his wealth of test-market data, improvement on this score will come through experience. Hopefully, he won't make the same mistakes twice.

Paradise Foods, on the other hand, must face up to a long-term problem with its corporate organization. The company should consider reorganizing its dessert group to end the division between new and established products. The structure of the Paradise dessert group is not uncommon. Nor are the biases such a structure can create. Established products are what generate current profits and cash flows. In a company like Paradise, they are also the products run by the most senior managers in the group. These people wield the big advertising and promotion budgets and all the power that implies. That leaves new products—the future of the company—in the hands of the most junior members of the group, who are also the people with the least clout.

It's been my experience that in these kinds of environments, new products often lose close calls to the established profit generators—and growth of the entire category suffers as a result. If Barbara Mayer were responsible for the entire category—both established and new desserts—she would have to be more of a new product champion and adopt a longer-term perspective on what's right for the company.

Finally, I would not encourage Bill to open more test markets. It's now time to move aggressively ahead of potential competitors. With some fine-tuning of the Sweet Dream marketing program, and a defense strategy for LaTreat, Paradise Foods may indeed be able, in Bill's words, "to have it both ways."

What I am proposing is prudent risk taking—which I define as intelligent people, who have done *enough* analysis to understand the fundamentals of a business proposition, moving forward aided by judgment rather than further study, with confidence in the organization's capacity to execute.

Good research means talking to customers

Bill Horton has collected a considerable amount of data in support of launching Sweet Dream. But the nature of his information and the way he presented it to the marketing committee virtually guaranteed a no-launch decision.

Let's first consider the substance of what Bill has collected. In all his months of research, Bill never seemed to explicitly address the one issue that most worried the marketing committee—cannibalization of LaTreat. In fact, there's no evidence that Bill talked with a single customer about how Sweet Dream was perceived relative to LaTreat. The BehaviorScan data suggest the two products compete with one another. But we know they're very different: one is a frozen novelty on a stick and the other is a cookie-layered ice cream sandwich. Perhaps Sweet Dream has certain characteristics—taste, texture, calorie content, etc.—that Paradise could emphasize to distinguish it more clearly from LaTreat, thereby reducing cannibalization. Unfortunately, Bill doesn't seem to know what they are.

RICHARD F. CHAY *is director of marketing research for the NutraSweet Company in Deerfield, Illinois.*

He does know how Sweet Dream performed quantitatively in terms of trial, repurchase, and market share in both test markets. But these results explain very little about why there is a market opportunity for Sweet Dream in the first place. Had Bill generated consumer attitude data on the frozen specialty dessert category in general, and Sweet Dream in particular, the marketing committee might have found his report more persuasive.

Which leads us to the next major miscalculation. Bill Horton submitted an overwhelming amount of information and analysis to a group of people with limited experience interpreting statistical material. Even after the committee rejected the Sweet Dream launch, Bill returned to his mountain of computer-based information and spent the weekend mining more statistical ore.

> **Why didn't Bill address the one issue that counted — cannibalization?**

And what does he do with the new data? He uses it to attack LaTreat. Bill's analysis of the product's faltering franchise seems persuasive, but confronting Barbara directly demonstrates little political insight. Bill obviously doesn't understand the culture of Paradise Foods. Nor does he seem to understand that launch decisions at most companies are made on more than just the black-and-white realities of market tests.

I don't see how Bill Horton can find his way out of the hole he has dug for himself. And that's too bad, because Paradise management clearly made its no-launch decision based on a false sense of security about LaTreat's long-term health. In a market category like frozen desserts, novelty is a critical asset — indeed, a prerequisite — for success. A company that wants to maintain a significant overall presence has no choice but to introduce new products on a regular basis, so as to recapture consumers as they tire of existing products. Paradise Foods missed this opportunity with Sweet Dream.

Reprint 88513

READ THE FINE PRINT

REPRINTS
Telephone: 617-495-6192
Fax: 617-495-6985

Current and past articles are available, as is an annually updated index. Discounts apply to large-quantity purchases.

Please send orders to
HBR Reprints
Harvard Business School
Publishing Division
Boston, MA 02163.

HOW CAN *HARVARD BUSINESS REVIEW* ARTICLES WORK FOR YOU?

For years, we've printed a microscopically small notice on the editorial credits page of the *Harvard Business Review* alerting our readers to the availability of *HBR* articles.

Now we invite you to take a closer look at some of the many ways you can put this hard-working business tool to work for you.

IN THE CORPORATE CLASSROOM.

There's no more effective, or cost-effective, way to supplement your corporate training programs than in-depth, incisive *HBR* articles.

Affordable and accessible, it's no wonder hundreds of companies and consulting organizations use *HBR* articles as a centerpiece for management training.

IN-BOX INNOVATION.

Where do your company's movers and shakers get their big ideas? Many find the inspiration for innovation in the pages of *HBR*. They then share the wealth and spread the word by distributing *HBR* articles to company colleagues.

IN MARKETING AND SALES SUPPORT.

HBR articles are a substantive leave-behind to your sales calls. And they can add credibility to your direct mail campaigns. They demonstrate that your company is on the leading edge of business thinking.

CREATE CUSTOM ARTICLES.

If you want to pack even greater power in your punch, personalize *HBR* articles with your company's name or logo. And get the added benefit of putting your organization's name before your customers.

AND THERE ARE 500 MORE REASONS IN THE *HBR CATALOG*.

In all, the *Harvard Business Review Catalog* lists articles on over 500 different subjects. Plus, you'll find books and videos on subjects you need to know.

The catalog is yours for just $8.00. To order *HBR* articles or the *HBR Catalog* (No. 21019), call 617-495-6192. Please mention telephone order code 025A when placing your order. Or FAX us at 617-495-6985.

And start putting *HBR* articles to work for you.

**Harvard Business School
Publications**

Call 617-495-6192 to order the *HBR Catalog*.

(Prices and terms subject to change.)

YOU SAID:

"Give us training tools that are relevant to our business...ones we can use *now*."

"We need new cases that stimulate meaningful discussion."

"It can't be a catalog of canned programs...everything we do is custom."

"Make it a single source for up-to-date materials ...on the most current business topics."

"Better yet if it's from a reputable business school. That adds credibility."

Harvard Business School Publications

AND WE SAID:

"Introducing the Harvard Business School Publications Corporate Training and Development Catalog."

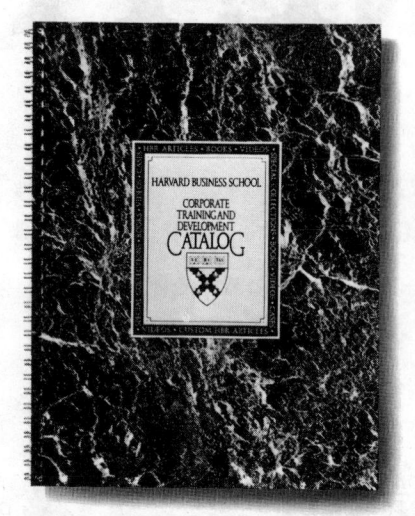

You asked for it. And now it's here.

The Harvard Business School Publications Corporate Training and Development Catalog is created exclusively for those who design and develop custom training programs.

It's filled cover-to-cover with valuable materials you can put to work on the spot. You'll find a comprehensive selection of cases, *Harvard Business Review* articles, videos, books, and more.

Our new catalog covers the critical management topics affecting corporations today, like Leadership, Quality, Global Business, Marketing, and Strategy, to name a few. And it's all organized, indexed, and cross-referenced to make it easy for you to find precisely what you need.

HOW TO ORDER.

To order by FAX, dial 617-495-6985. Or call 617-495-6192. Please mention telephone order code 132A. Or send this coupon with your credit card information to: HBS Publications Corporate Training and Development Catalog, Harvard Business School Publishing Division, Operations Department, Boston, MA 02163. **All orders must be prepaid.**

Order No.	Title	Qty. ×	Price +	Shipping* =	Total
39001	Catalog		$8		

Prices and terms subject to change.
*For orders outside Continental U.S.: 20% for surface delivery. Allow 3-6 months. *Express Deliveries* billed at cost; all foreign orders not designating express delivery will be sent by surface mail.

☐ VISA ☐ American Express ☐ MasterCard

Card Number_____ Exp. Date_____

Signature_____

Telephone_____ FAX_____

Name_____

Organization_____

Street_____

City_____ State/Zip_____

Country_____ ☐ Home Address ☐ Organization Address

Please Reference Telephone Order Code 132A